I0442703

I am grateful to God for everything! And I believe that the meaning of life is to make sense of other lives. C.A., you are the meaning of my life.
Lov U

VICTORIA LIMA
2024

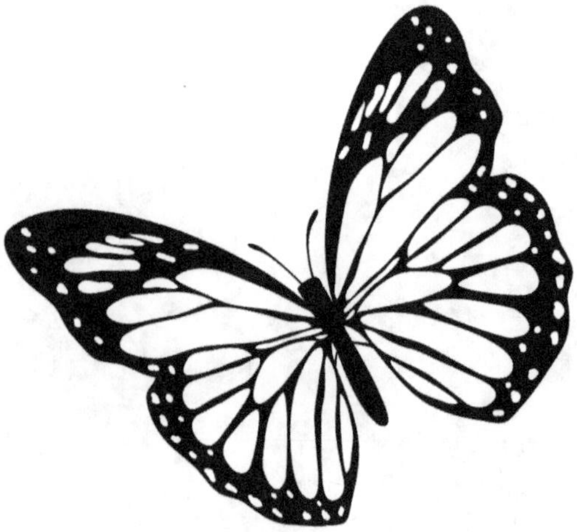

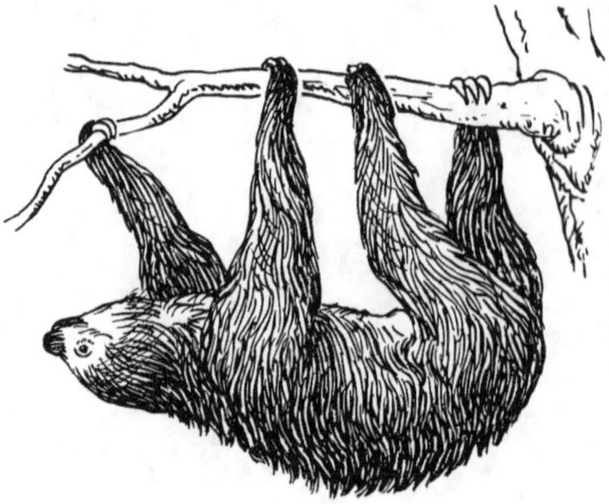

This Book Belongs to:

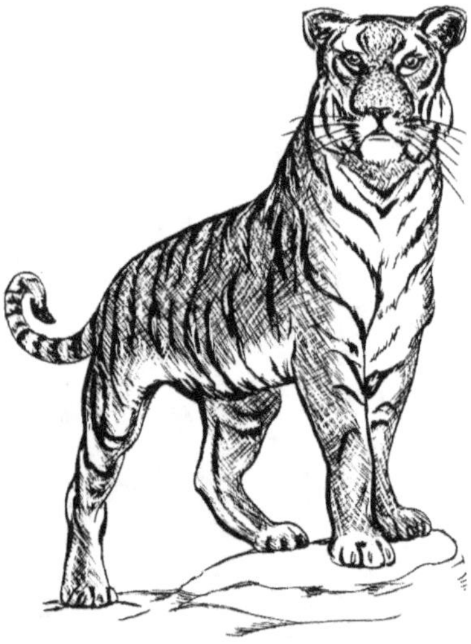

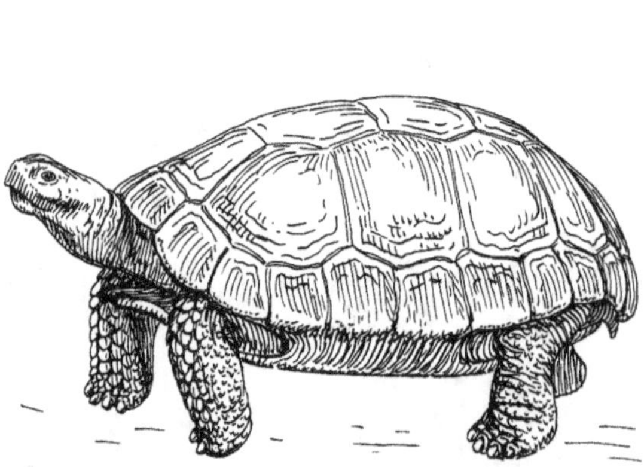

V.L.P©
Victoria's Lima publications

Test Color Page

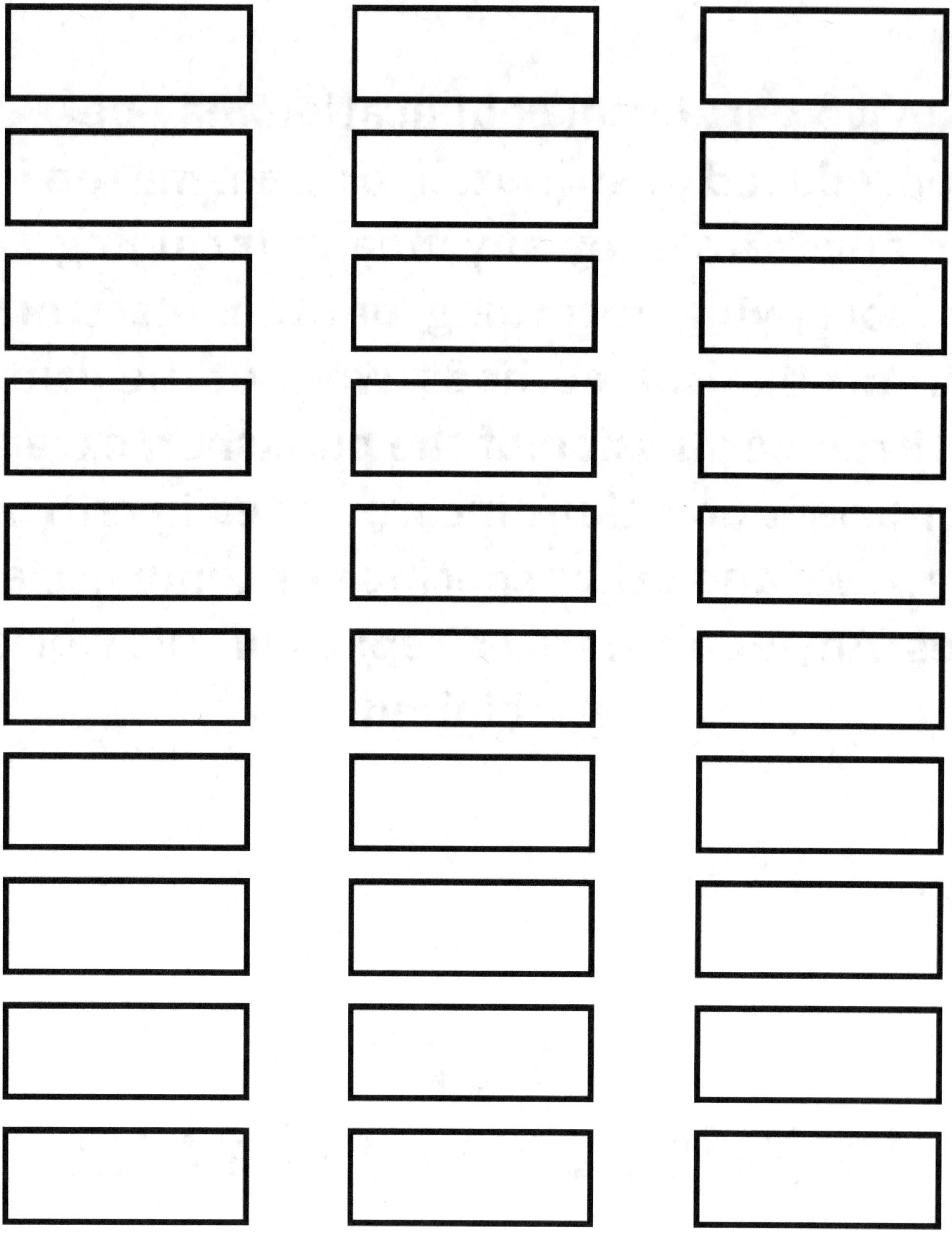

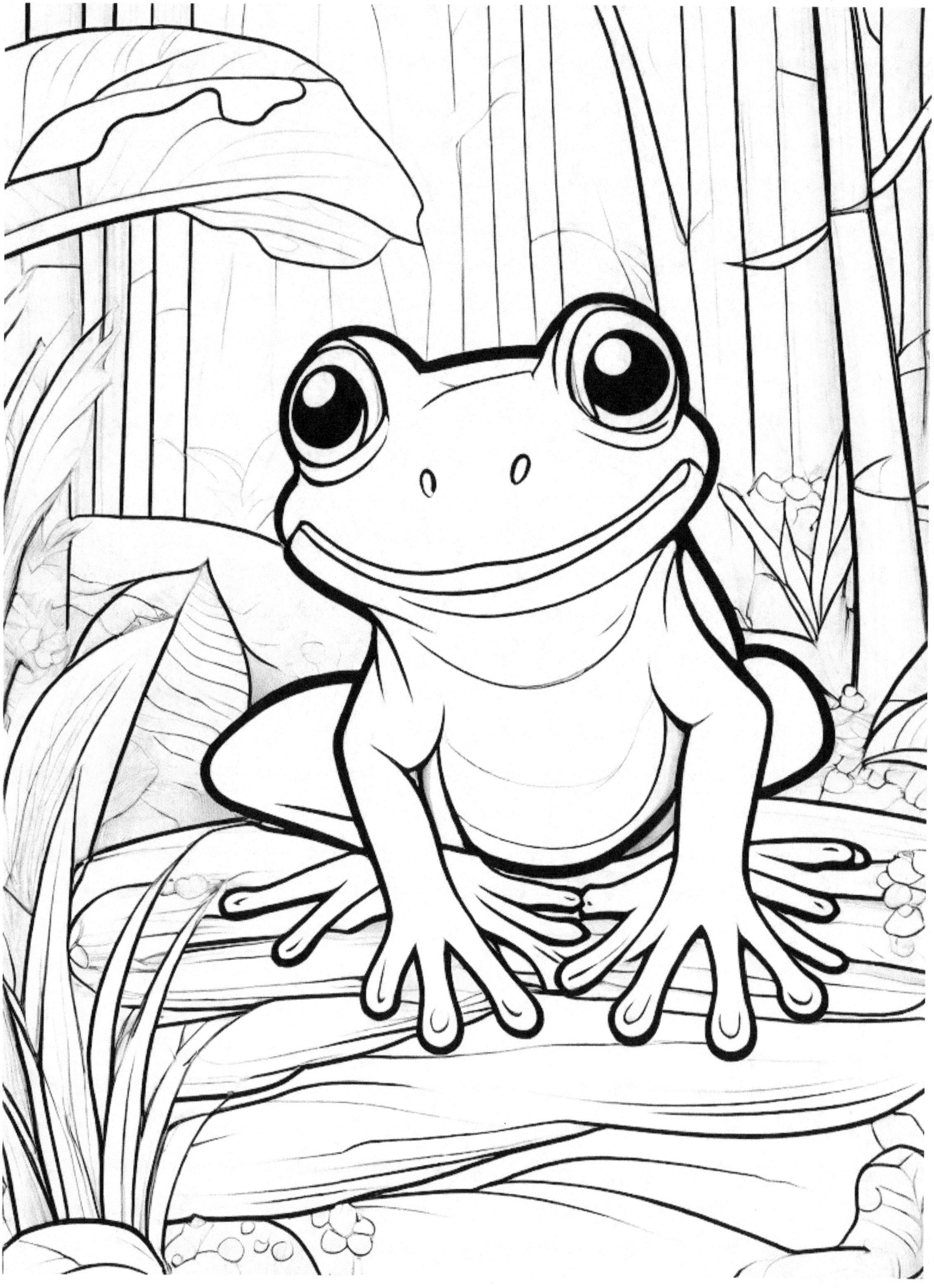

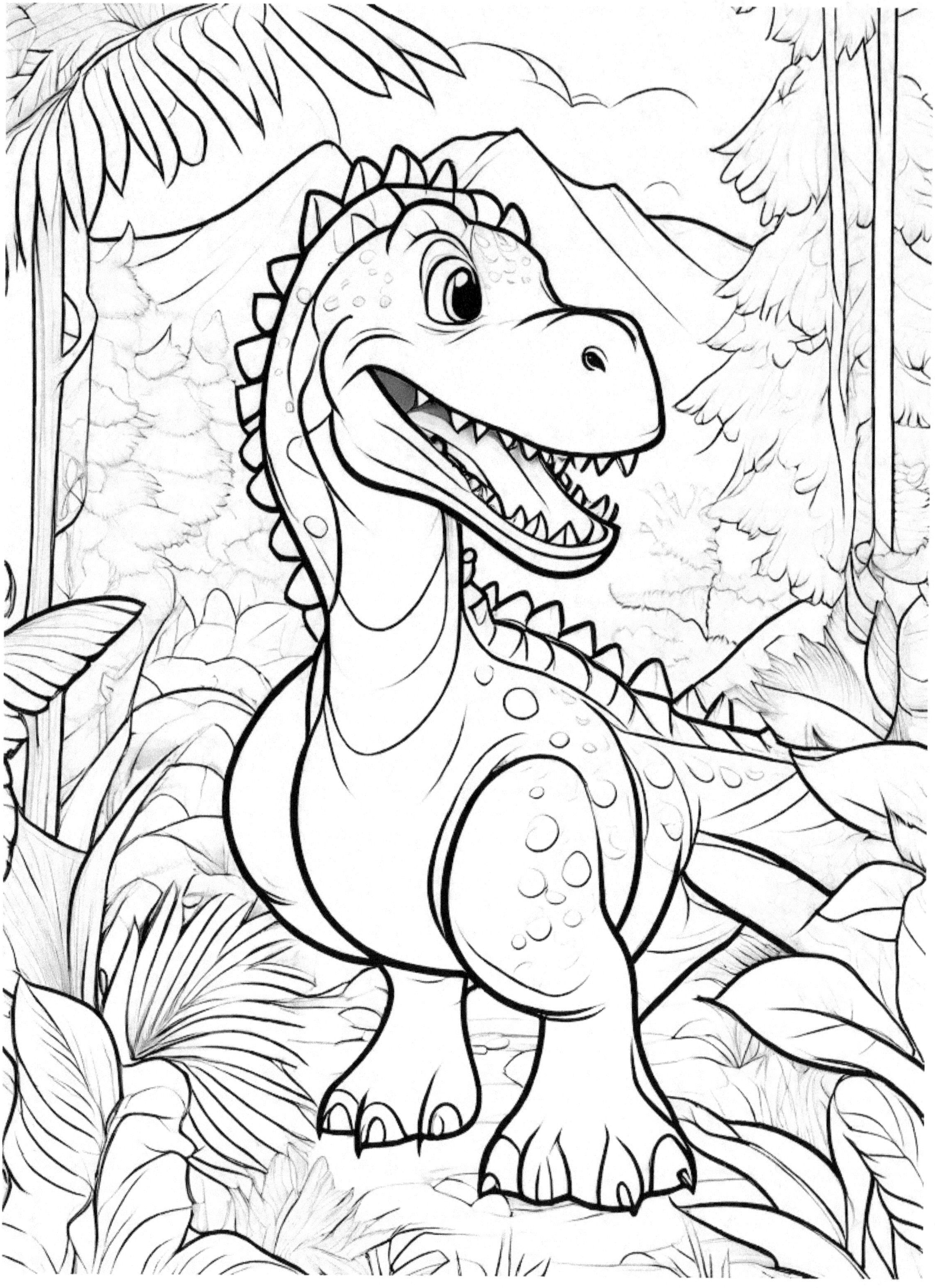

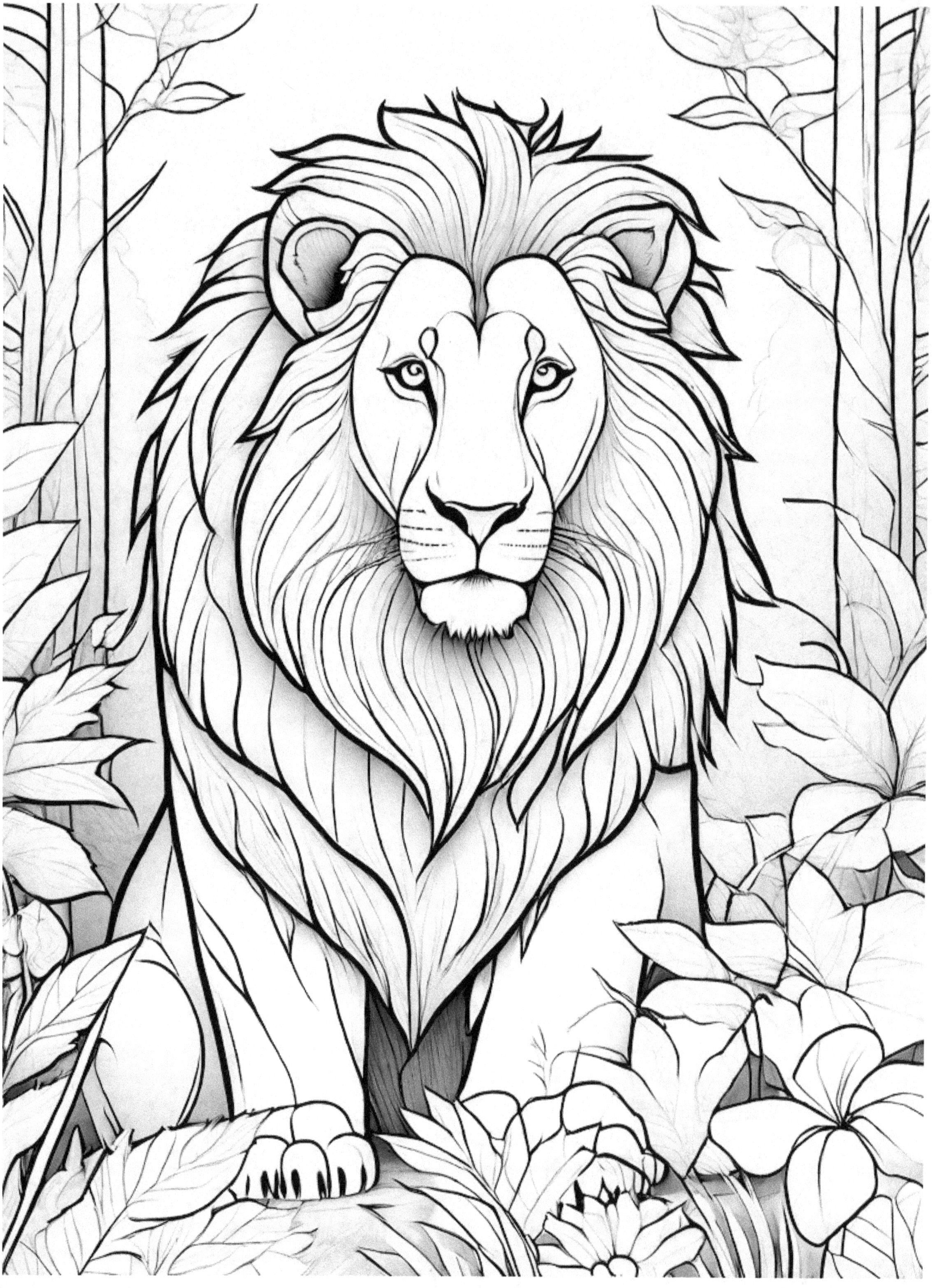

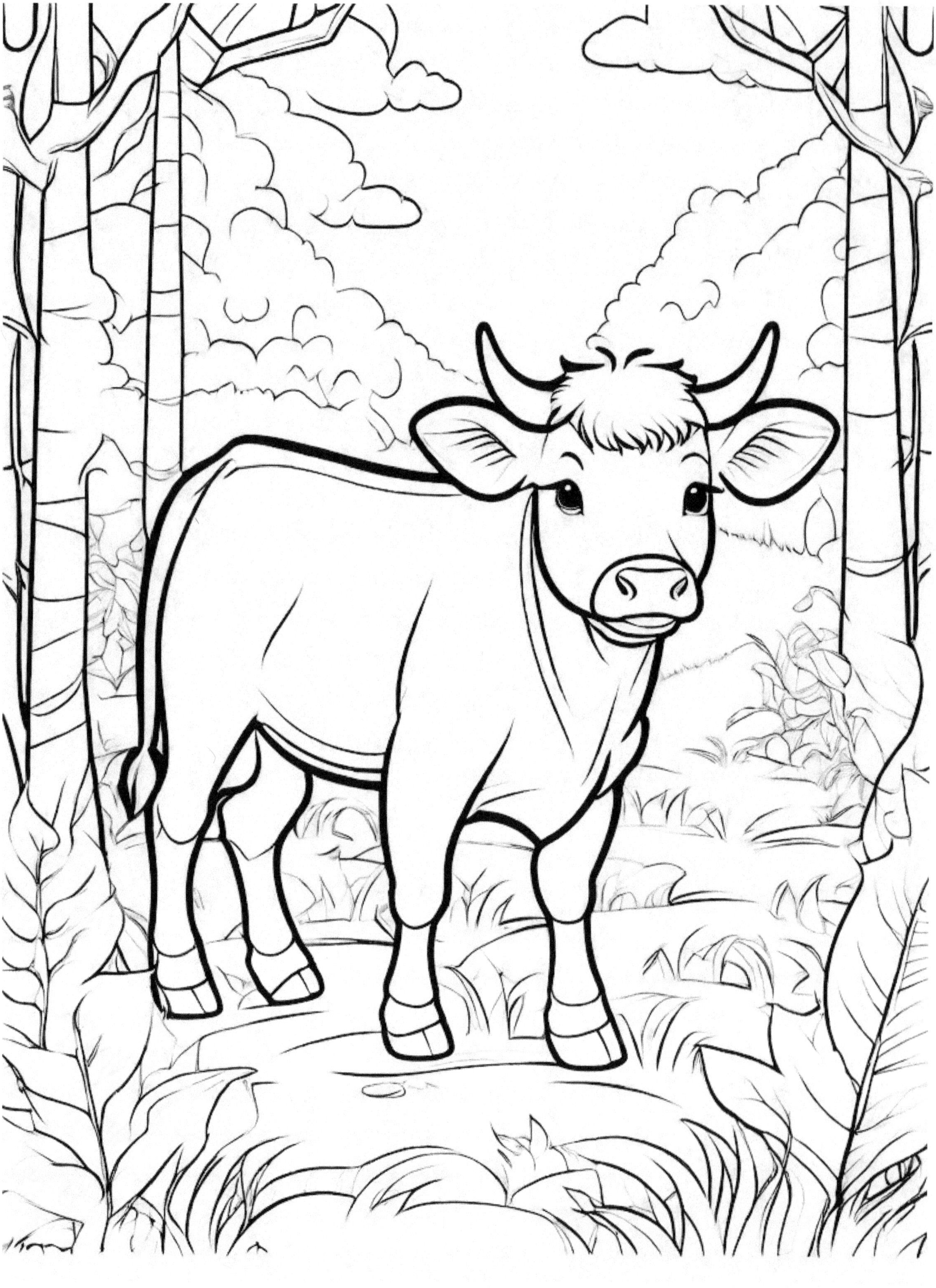

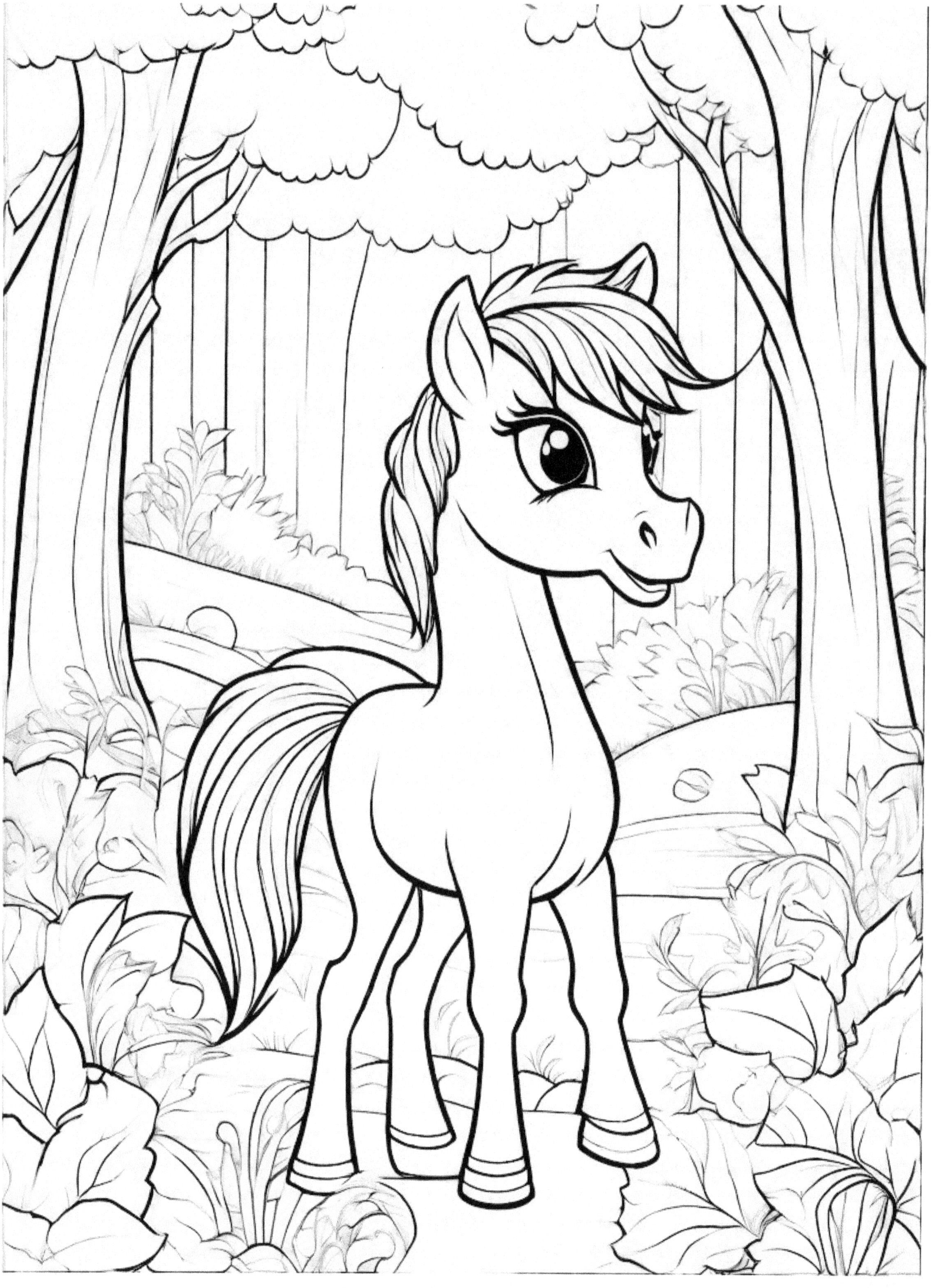

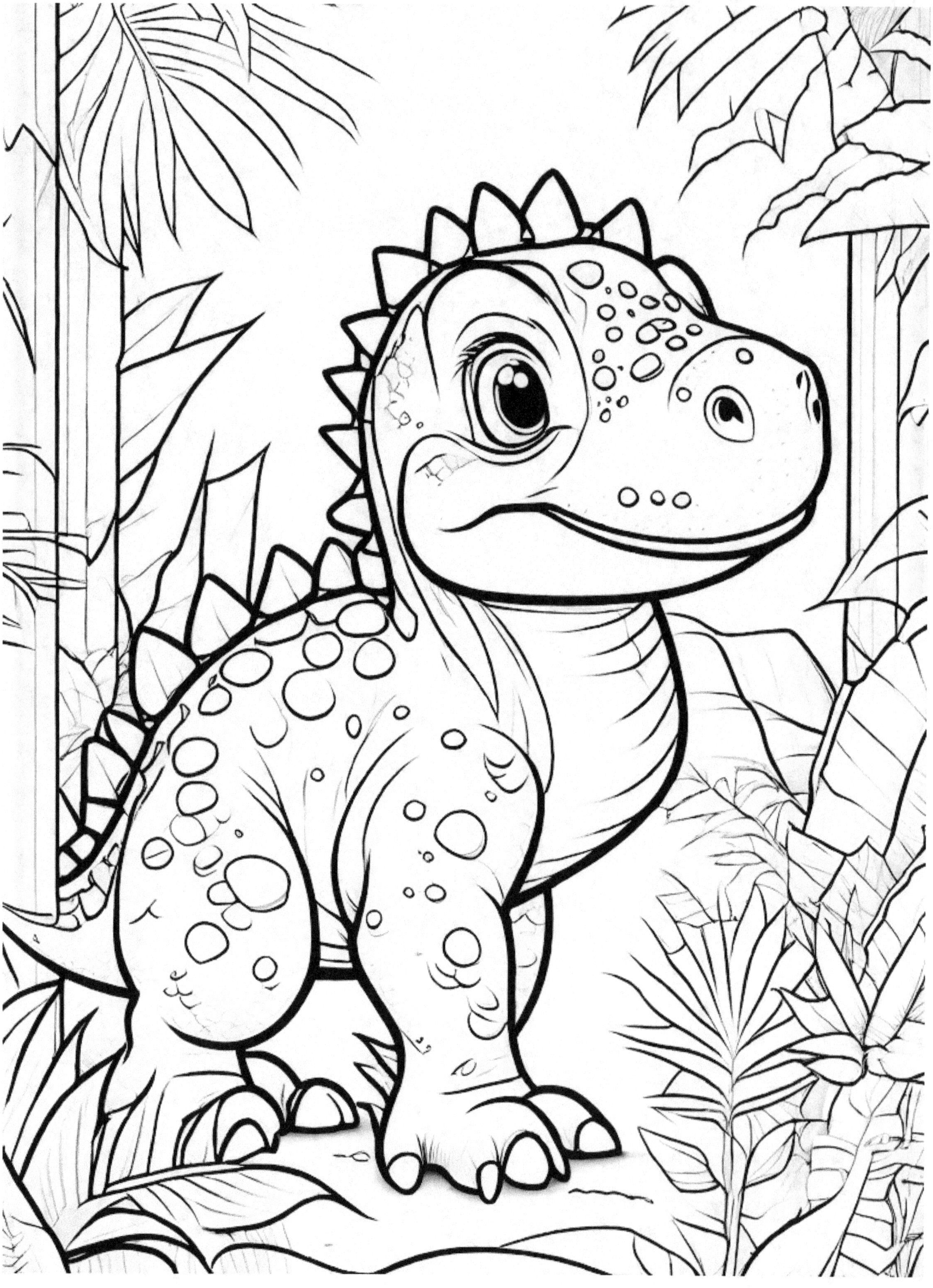

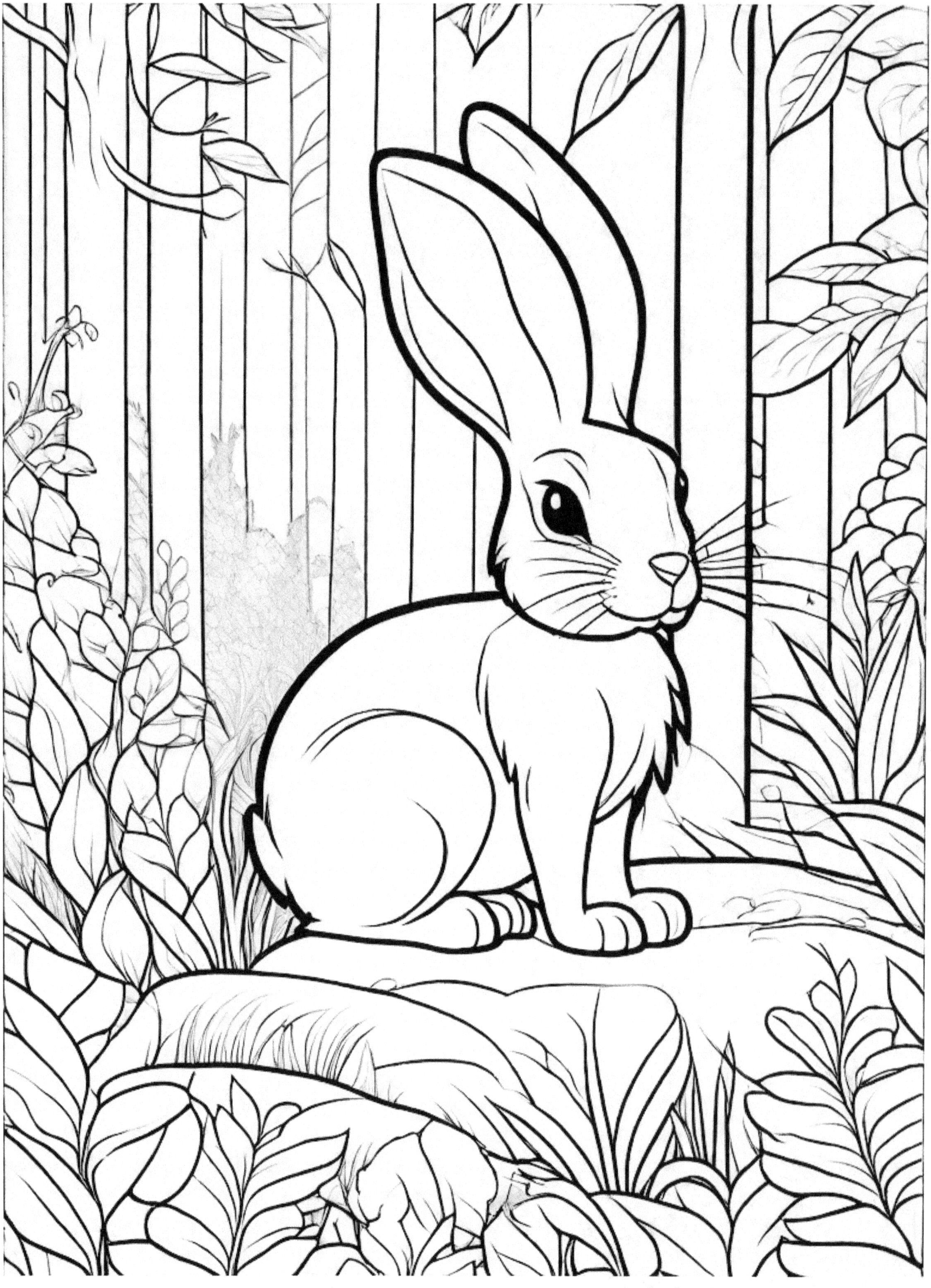

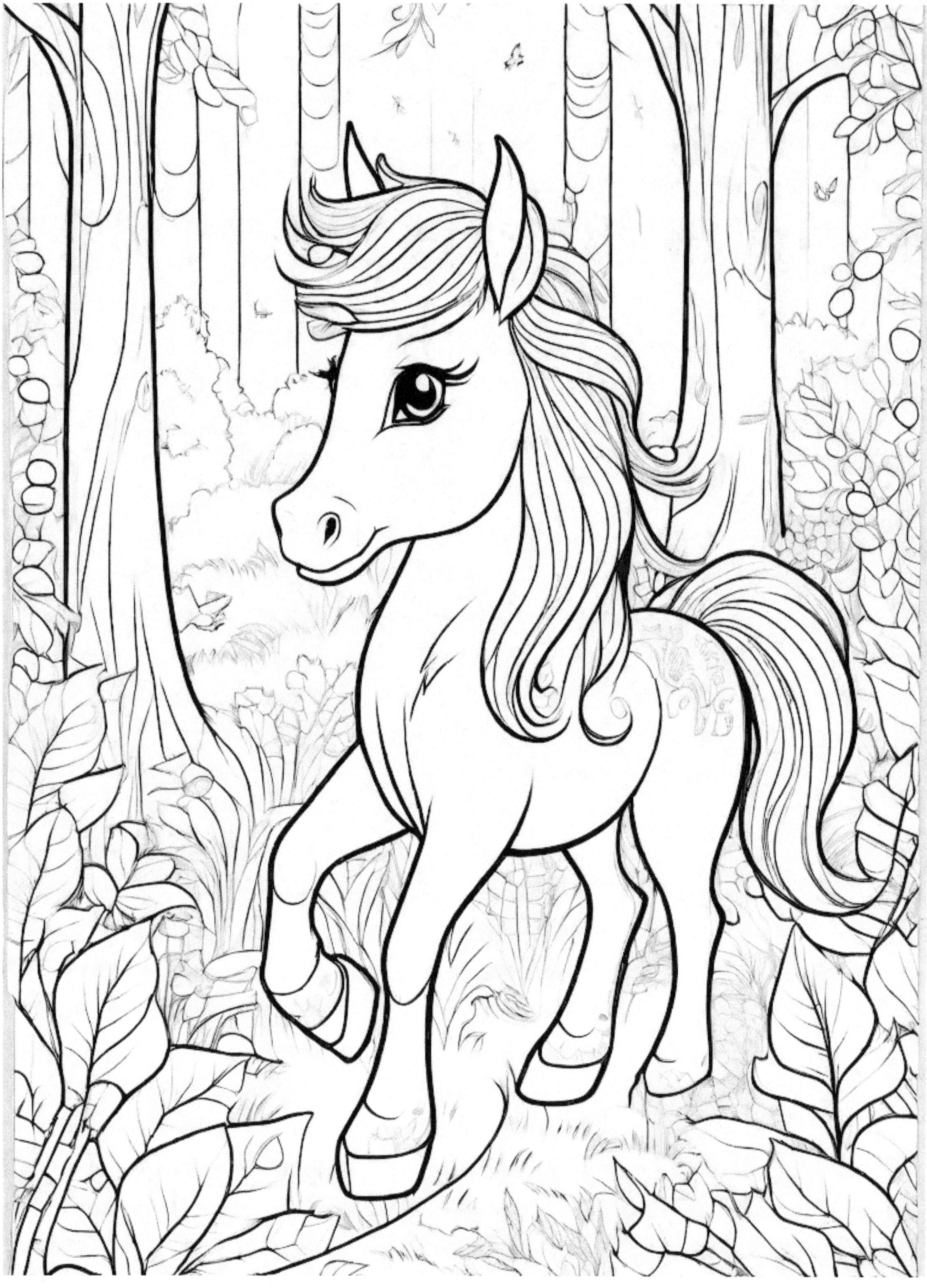

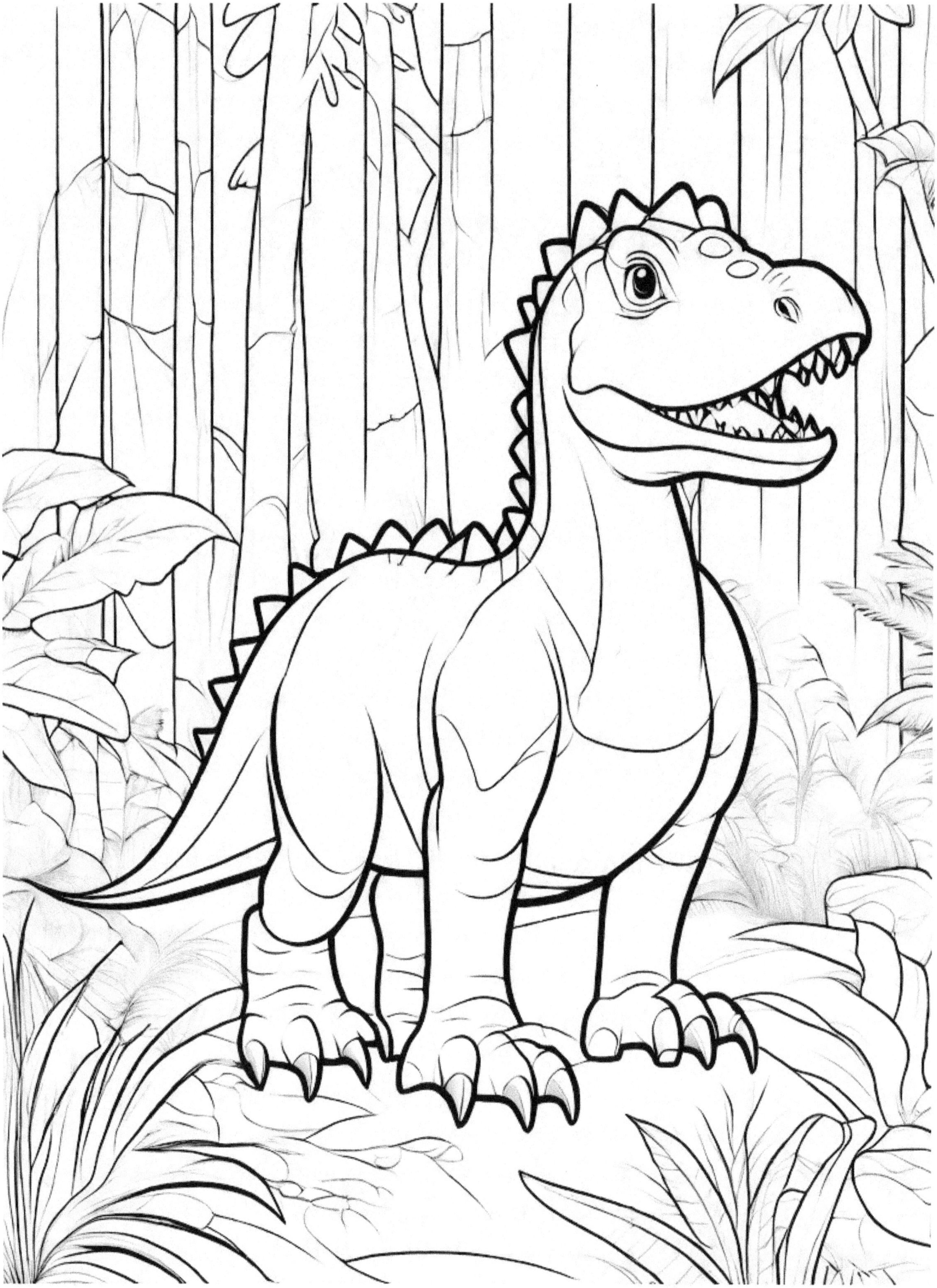

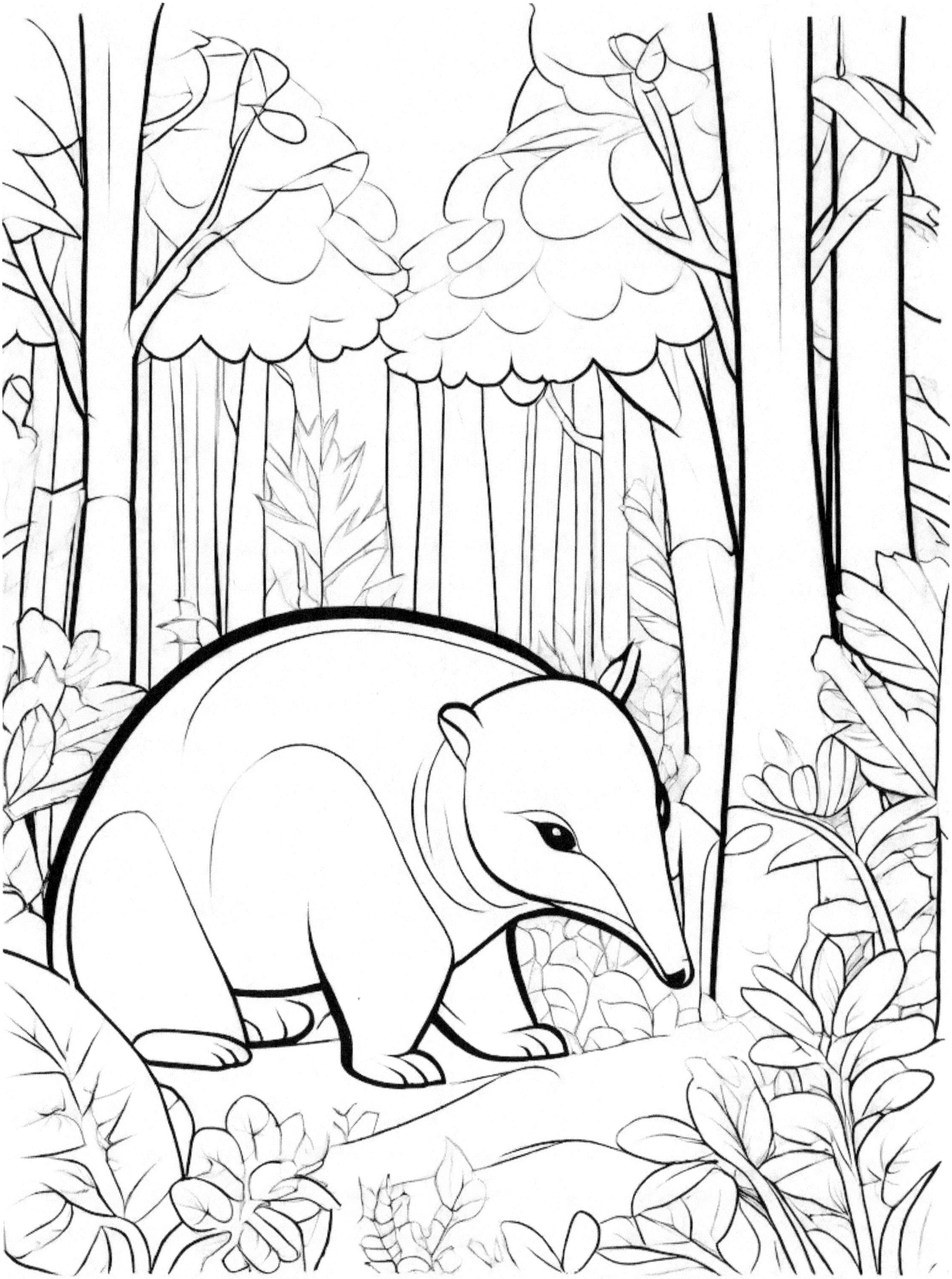

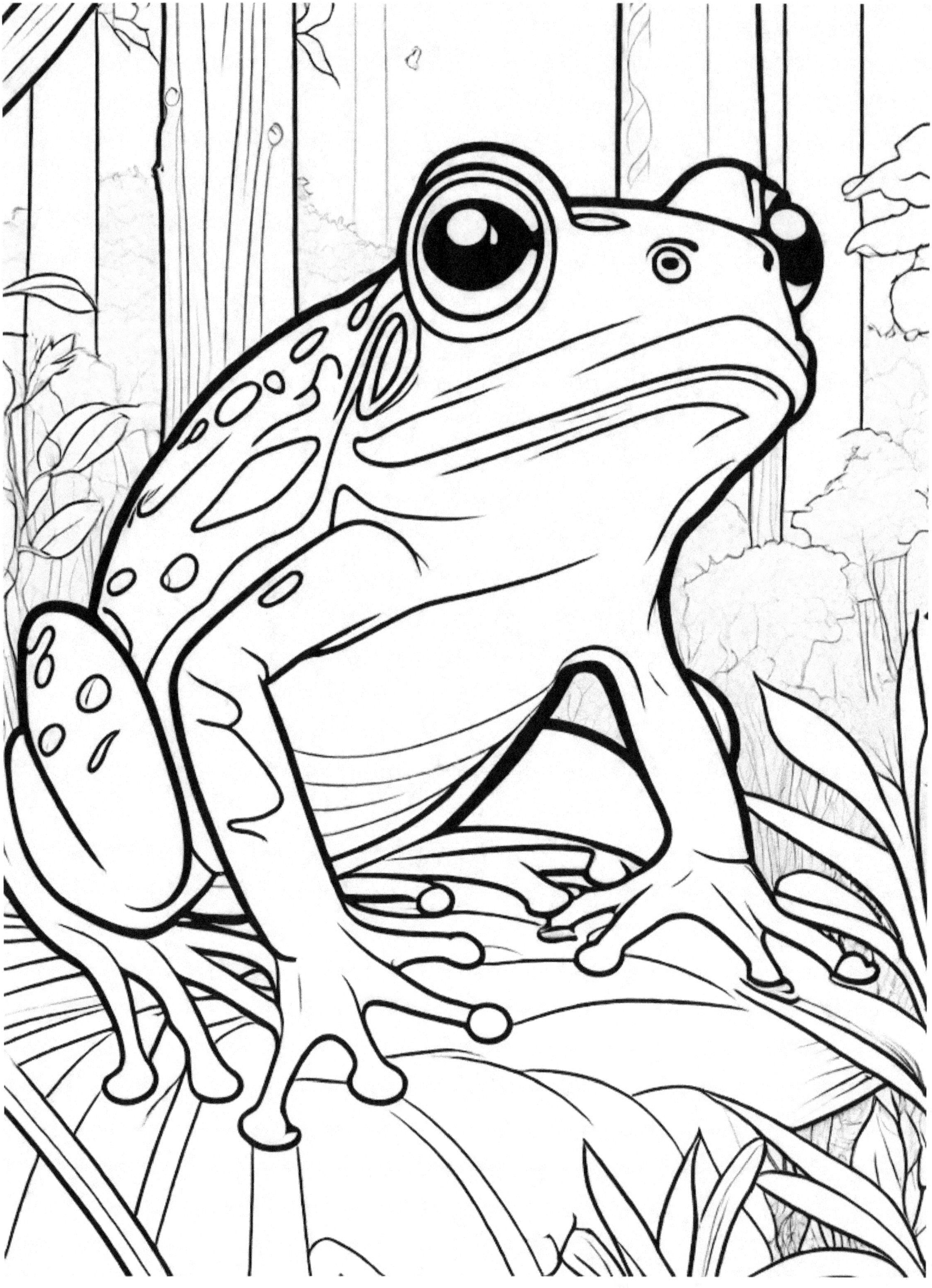

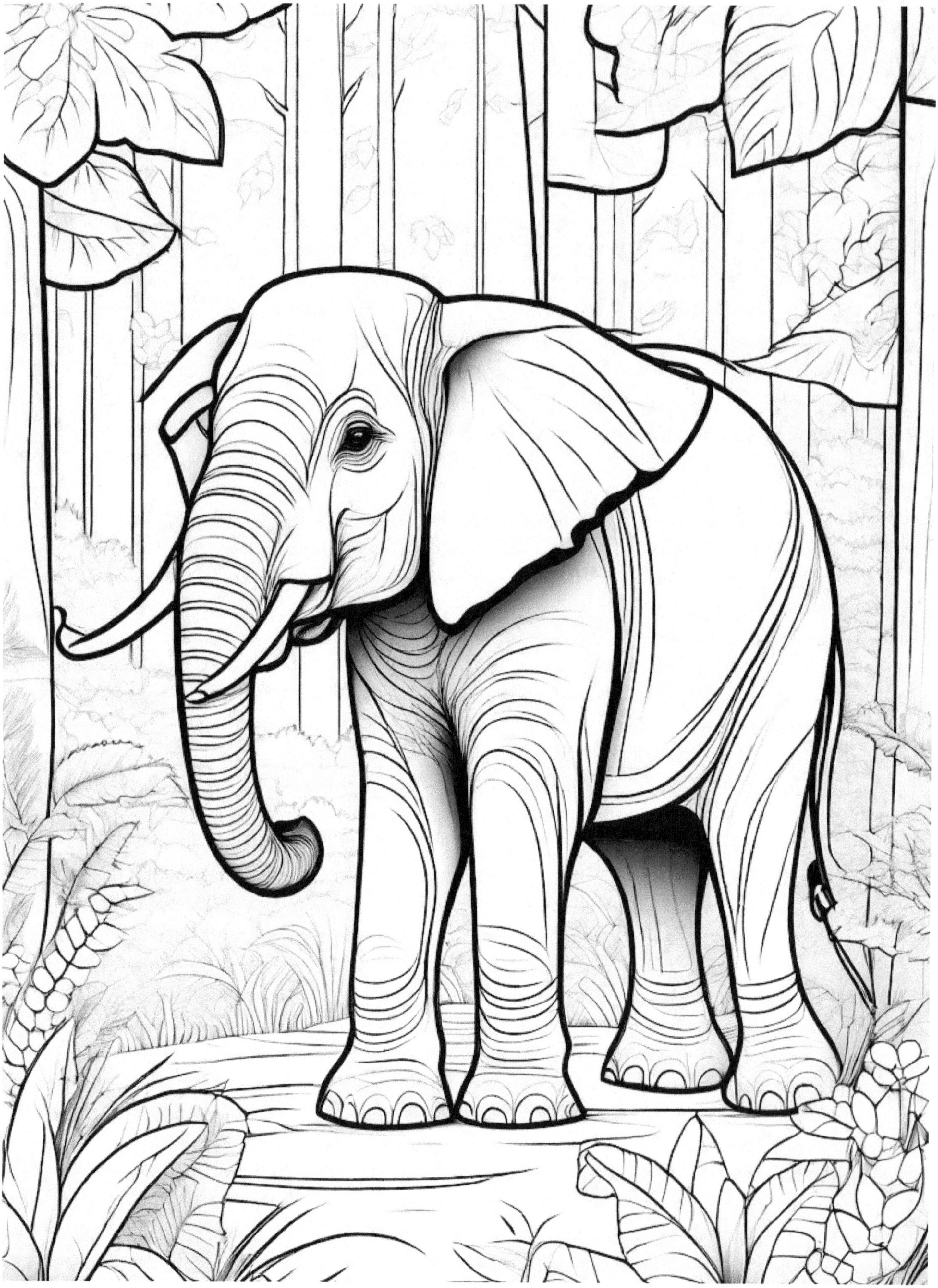

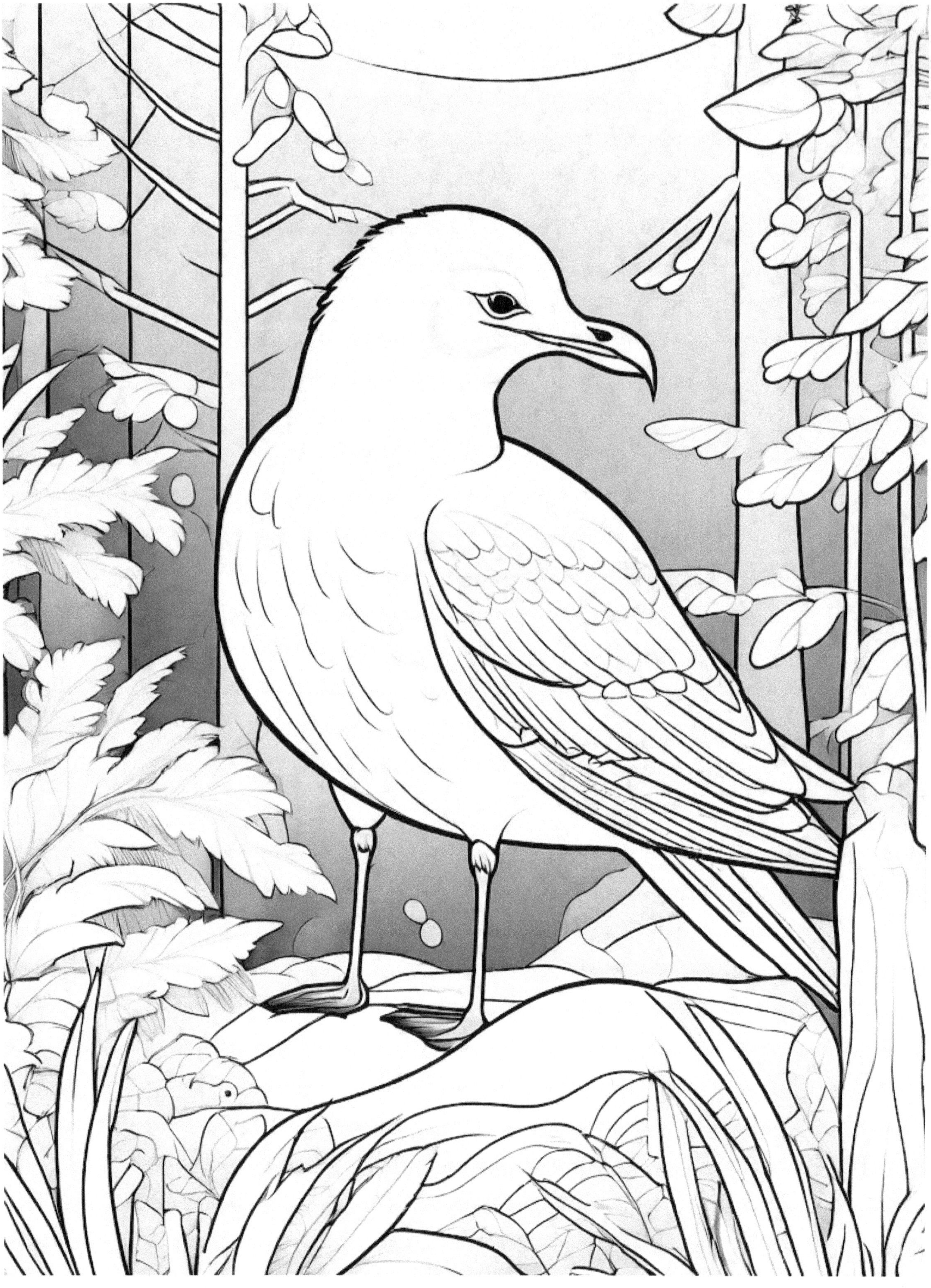

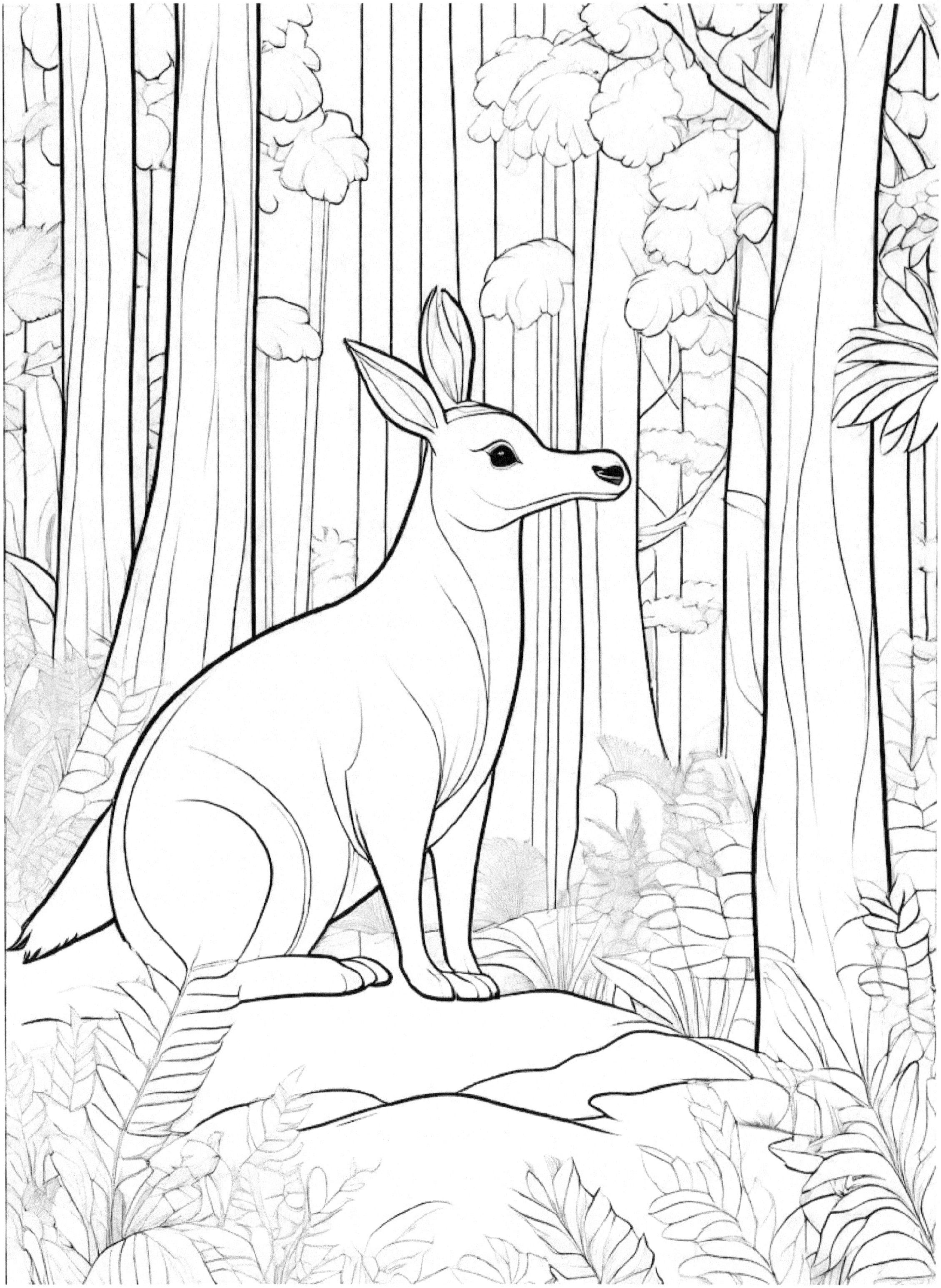

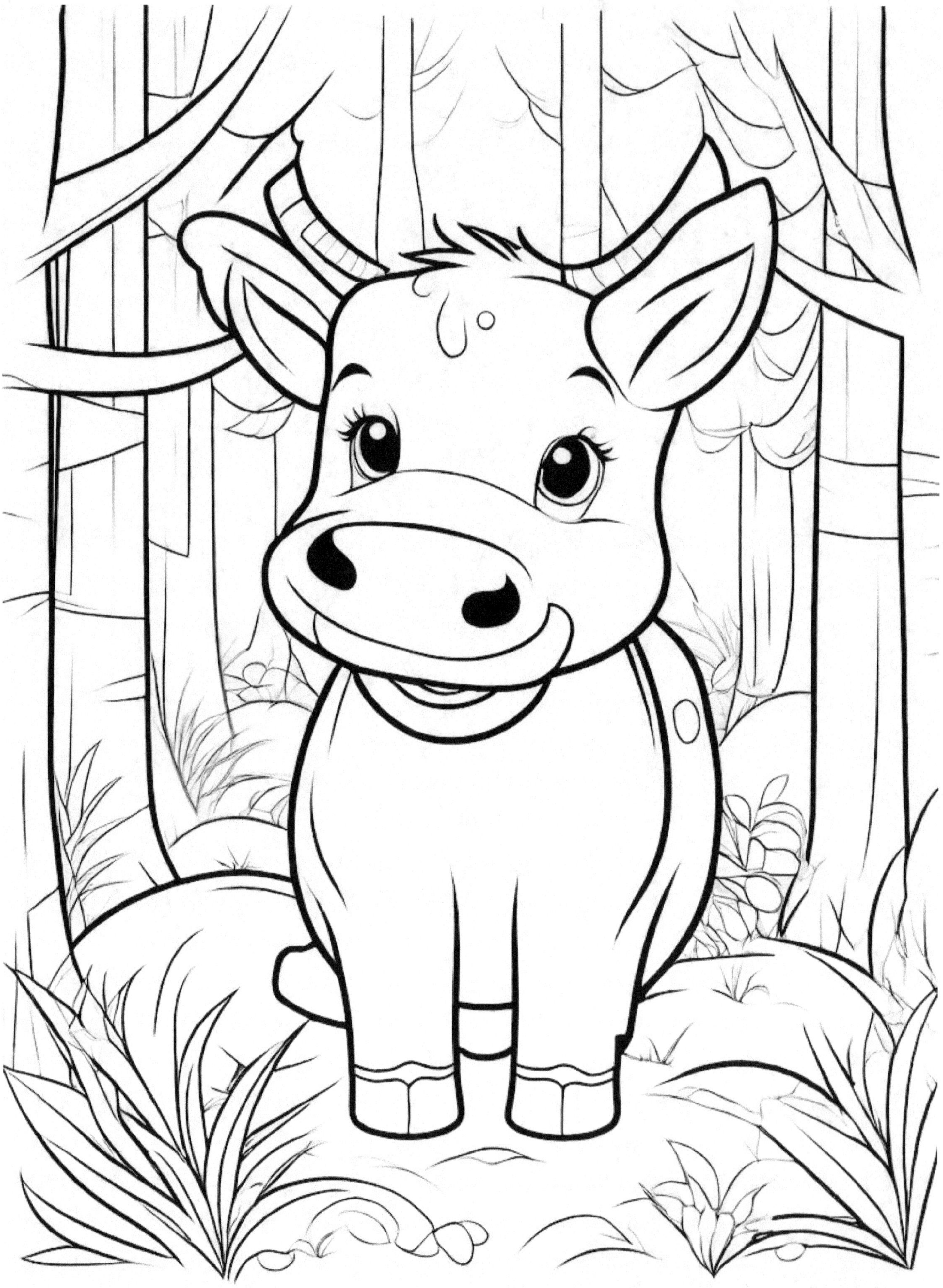

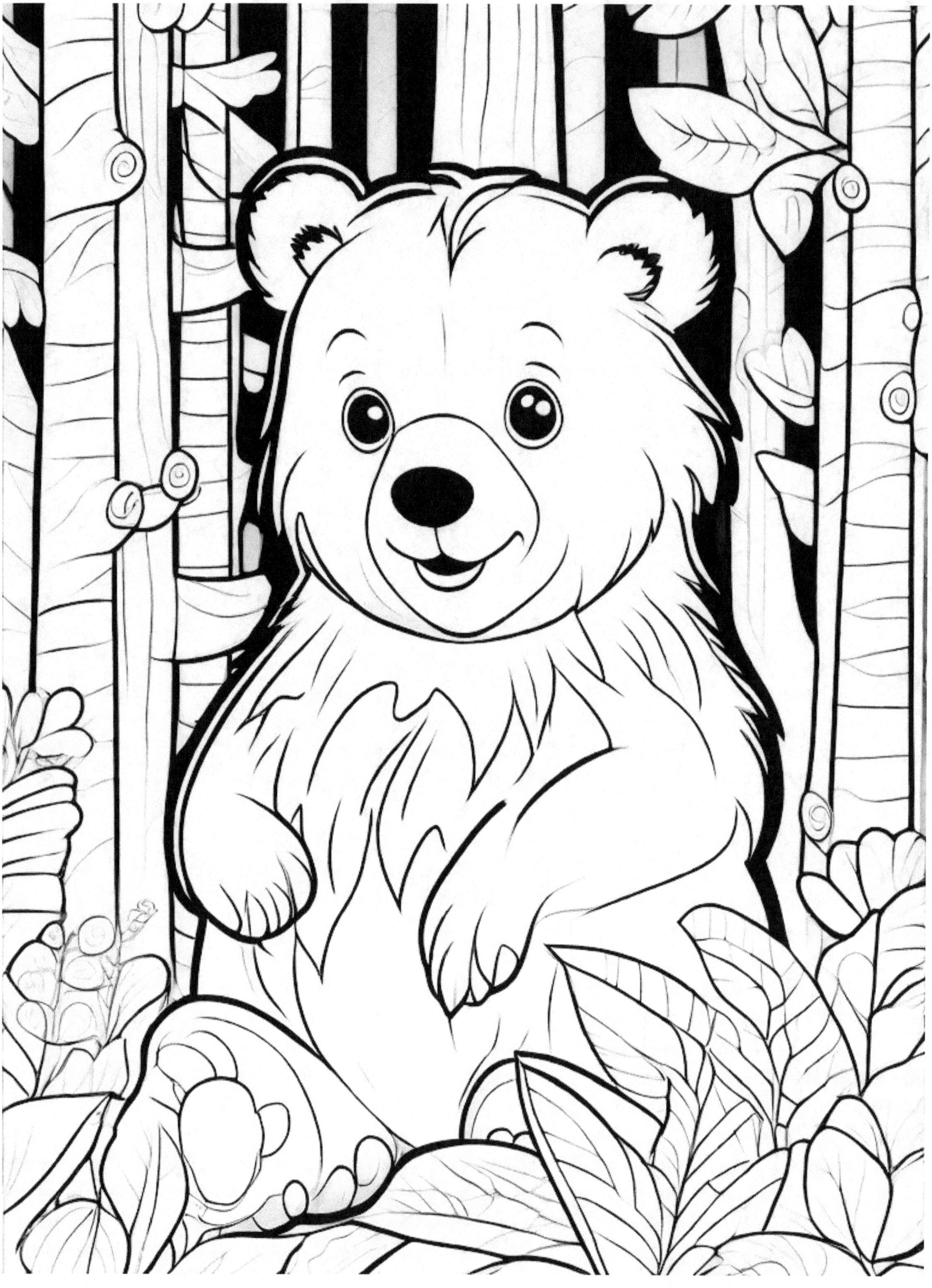

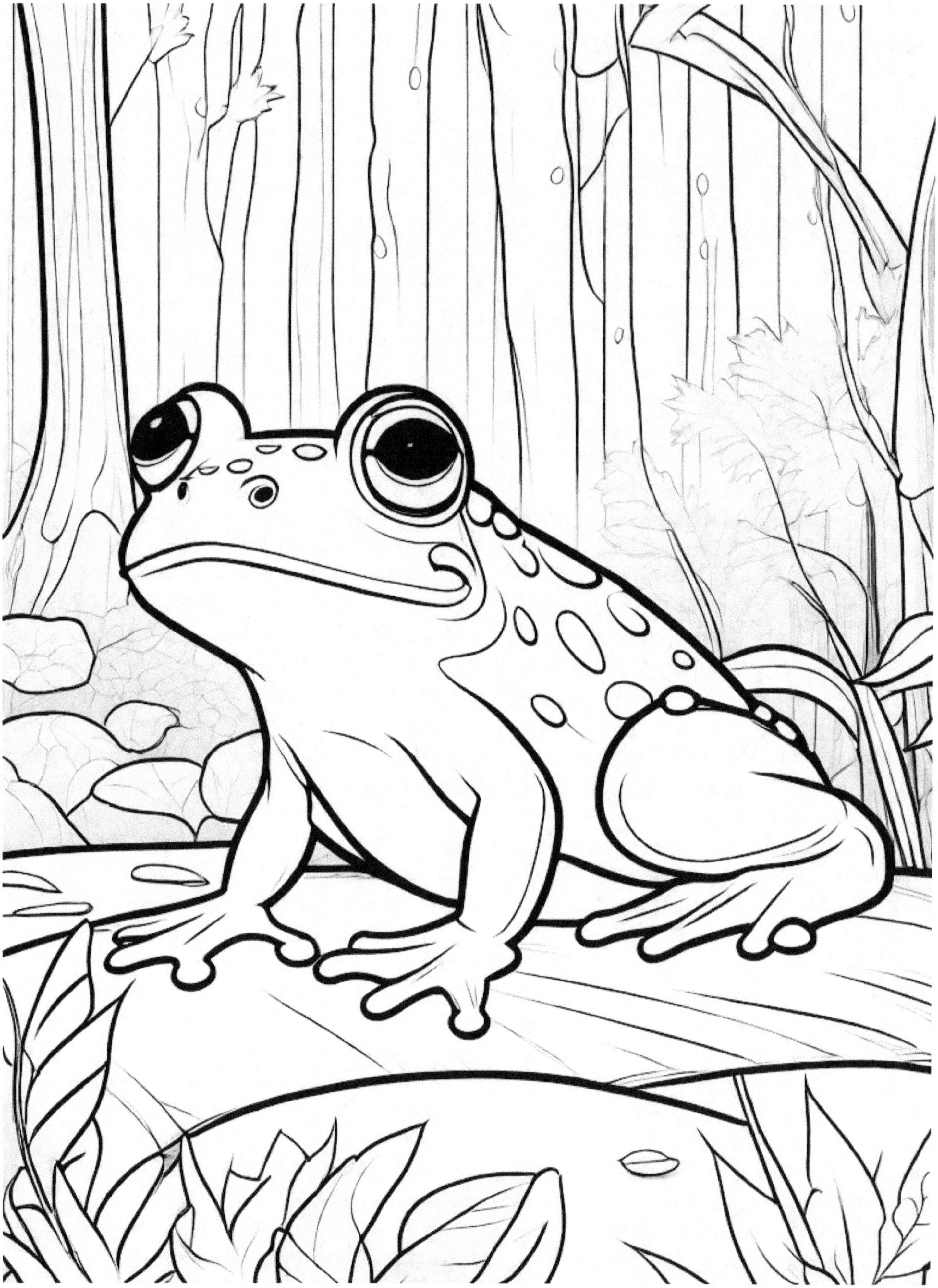

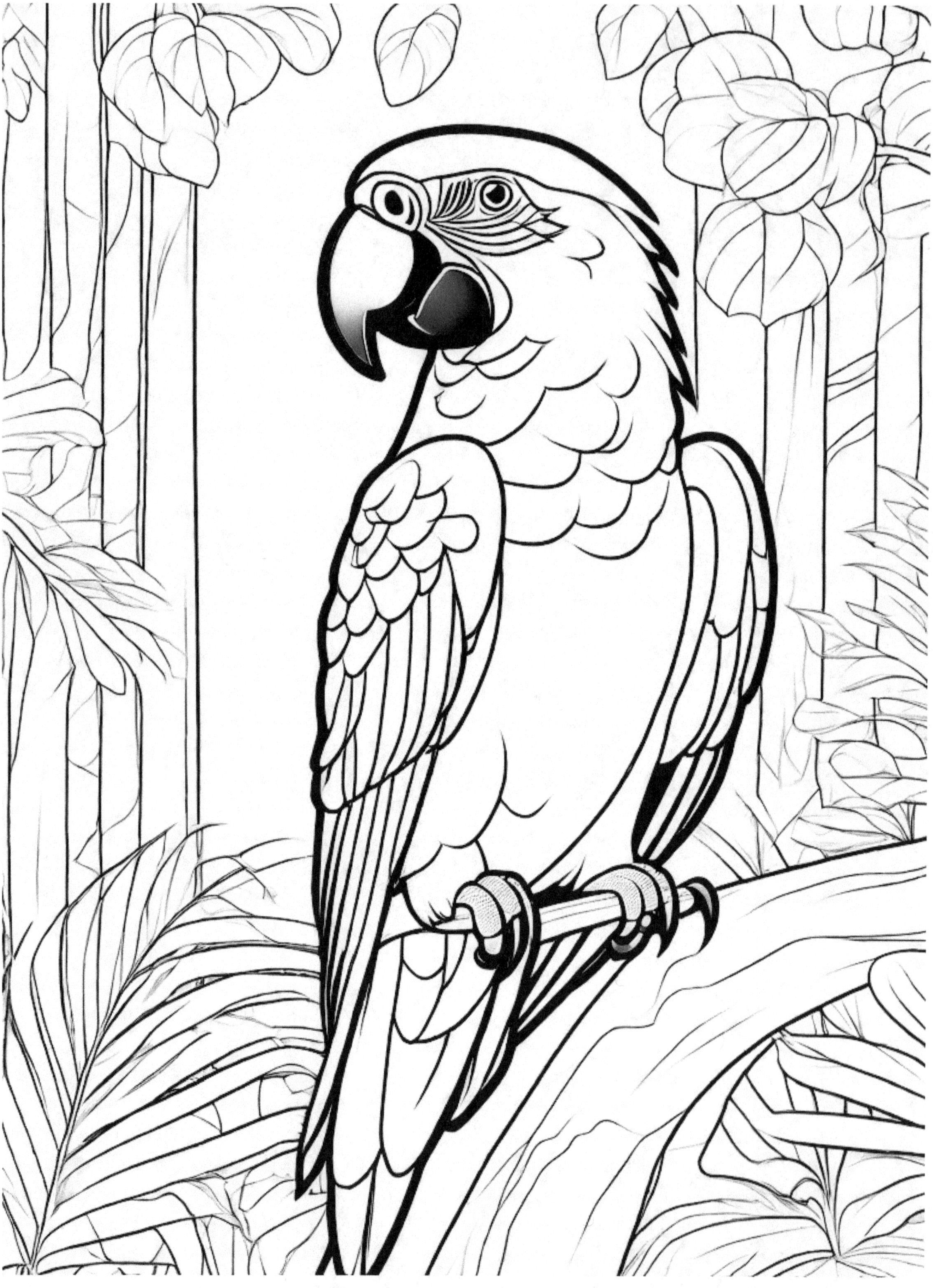

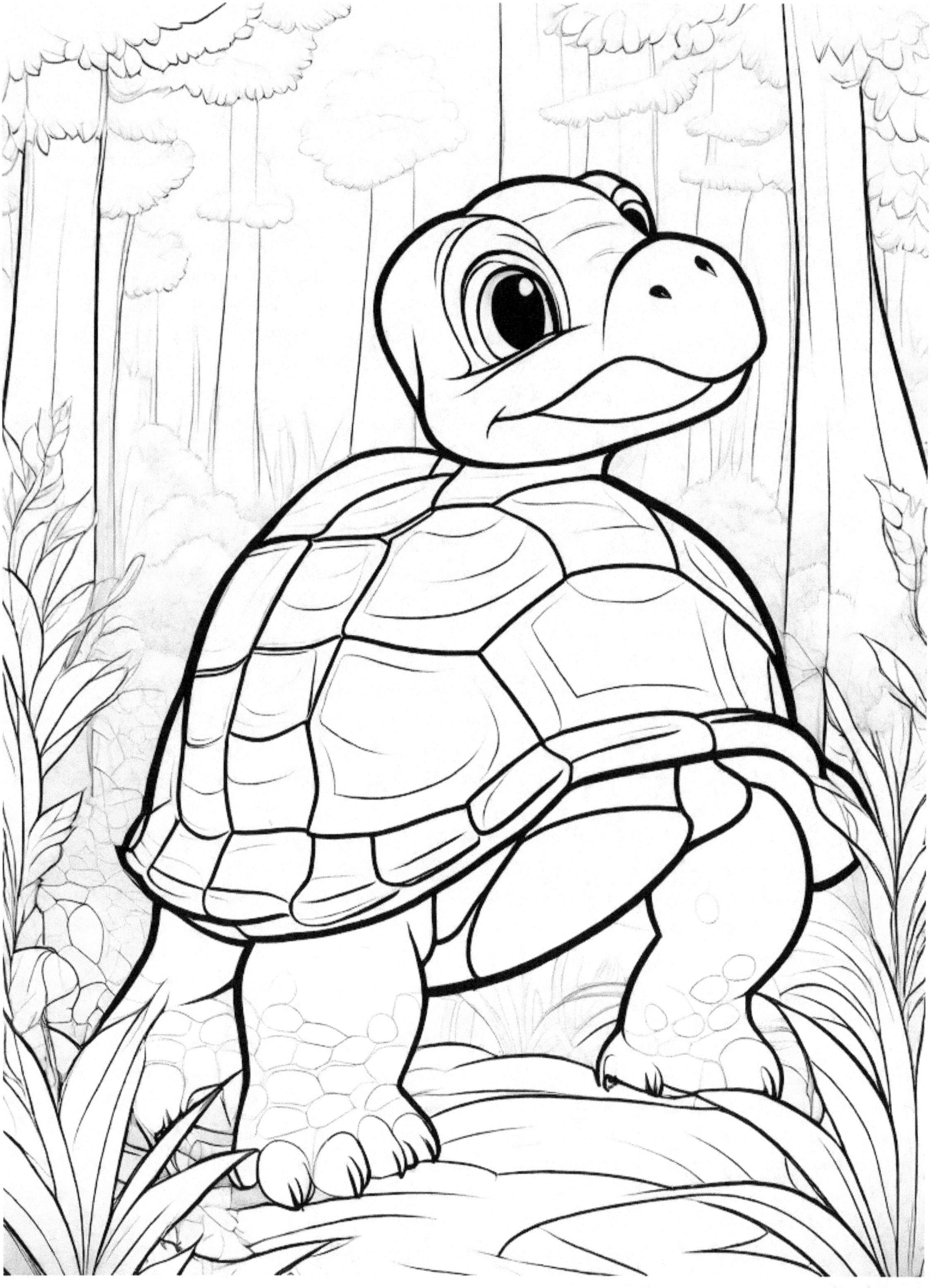

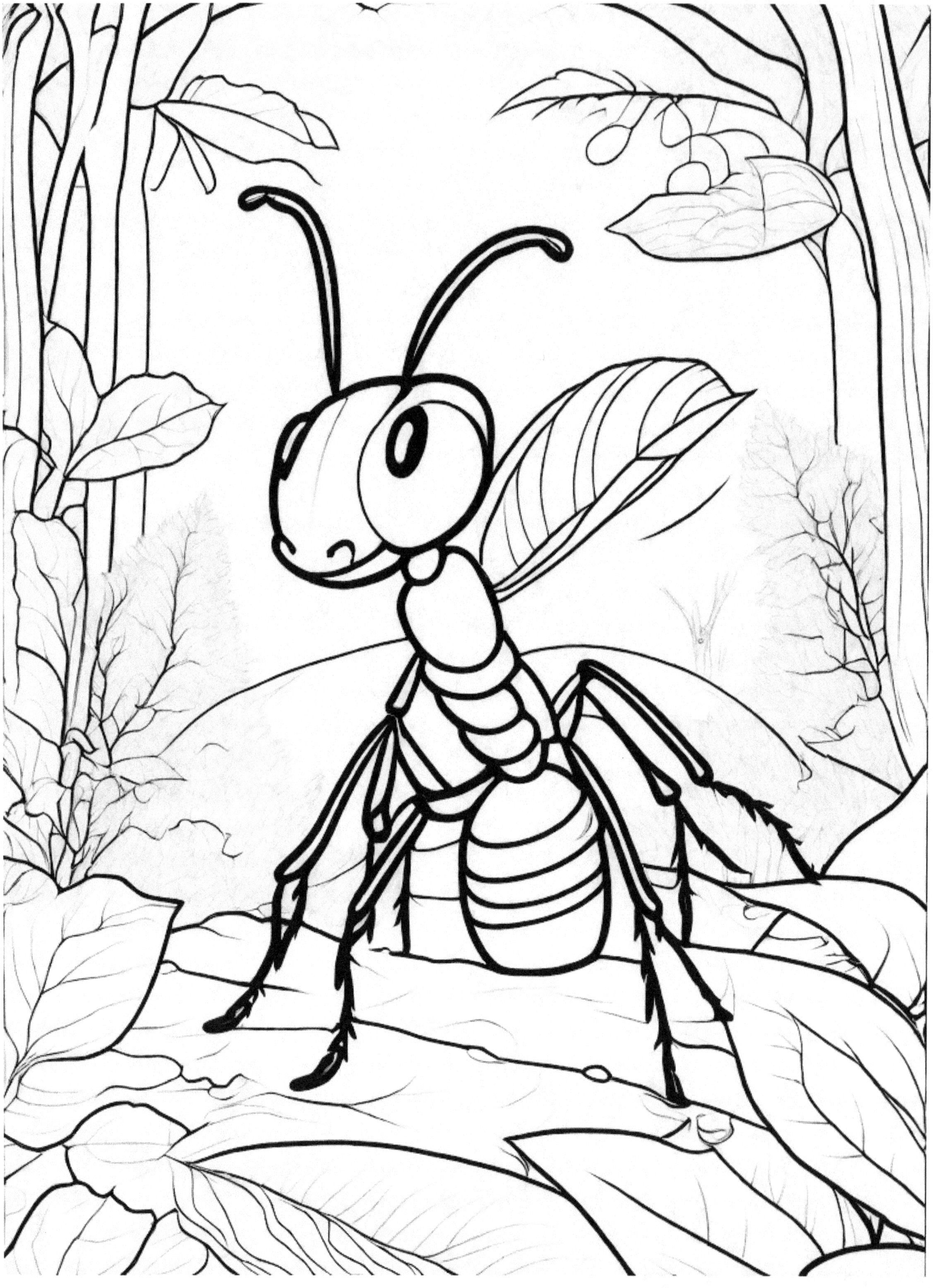

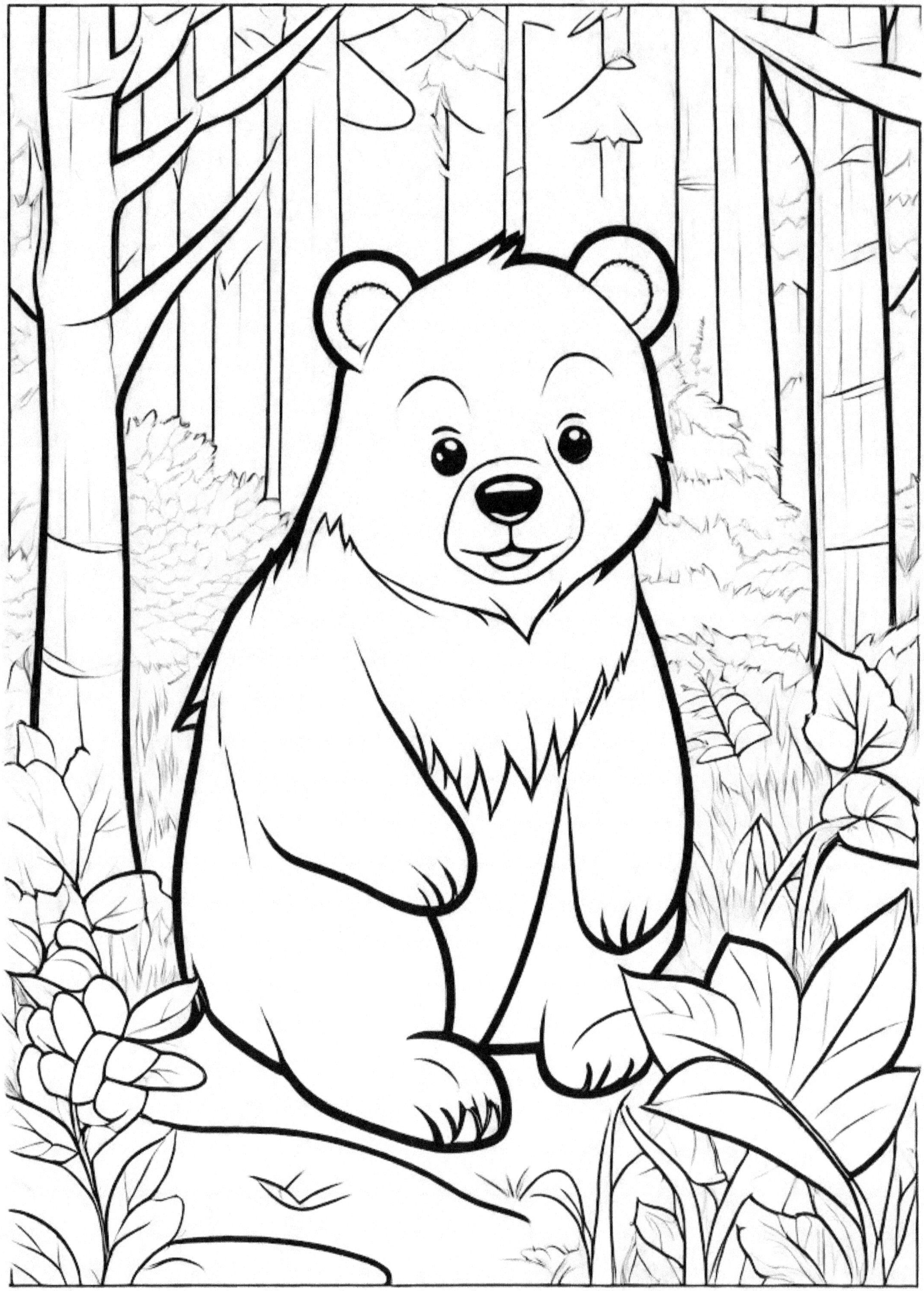

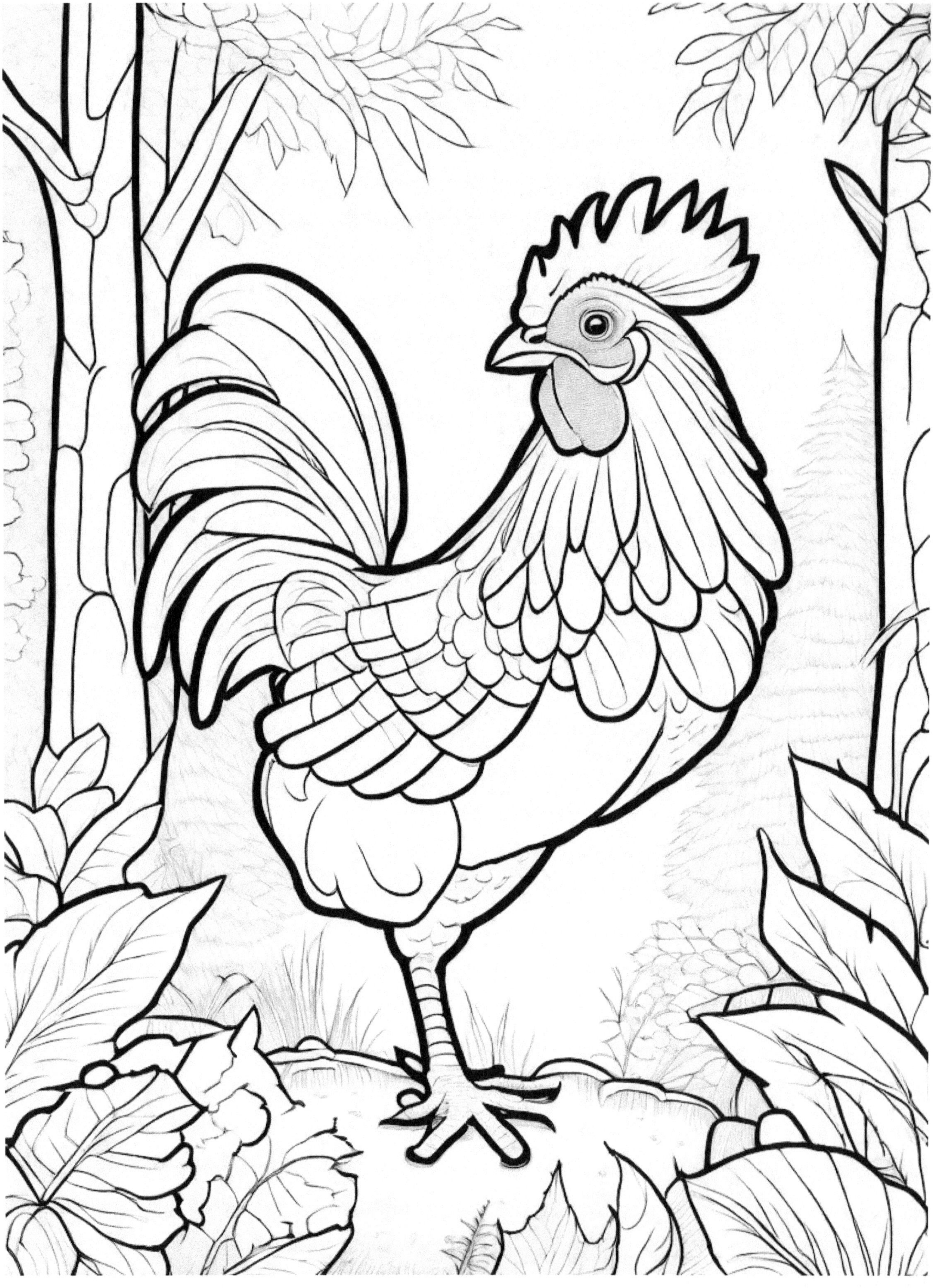

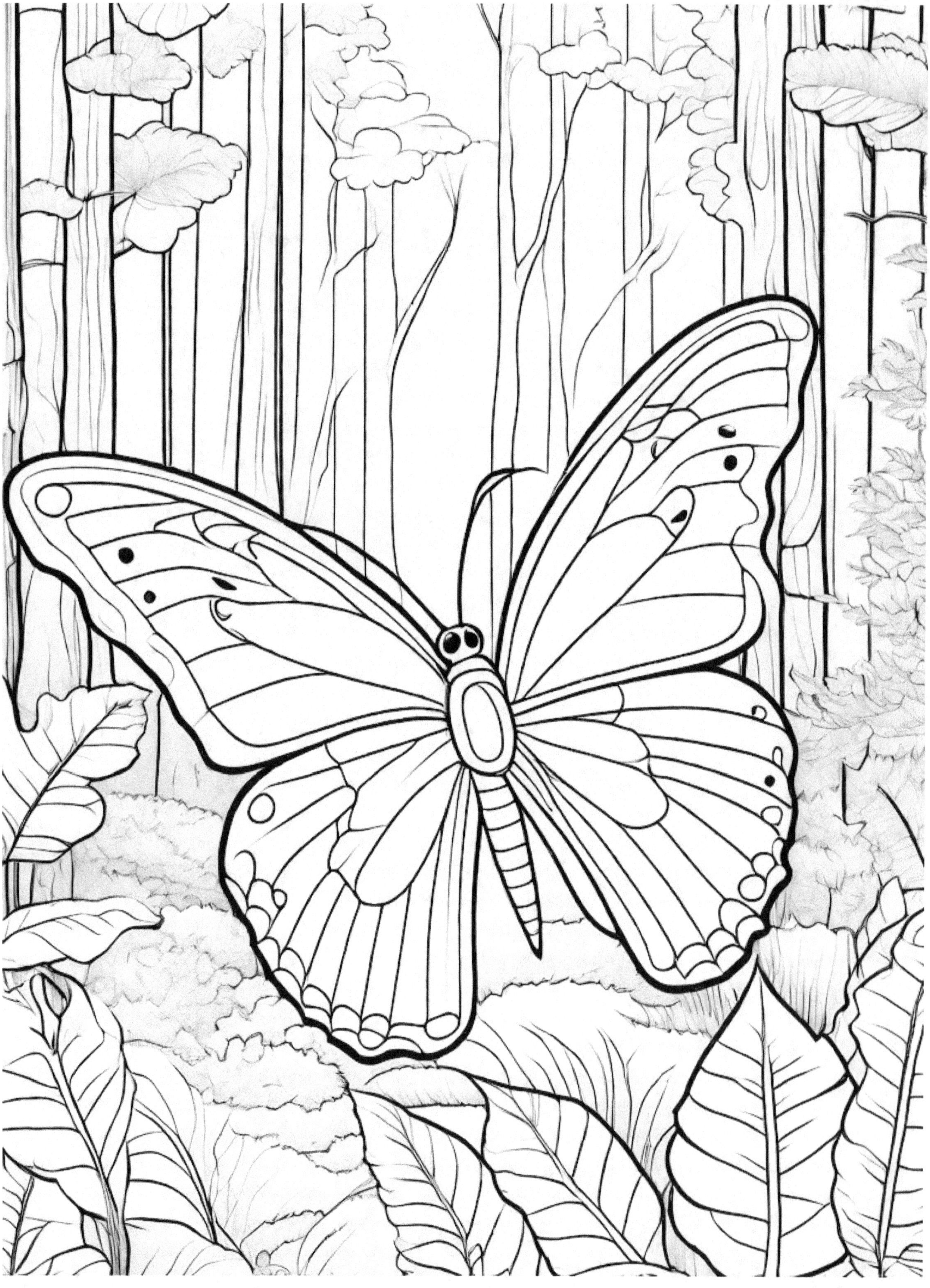

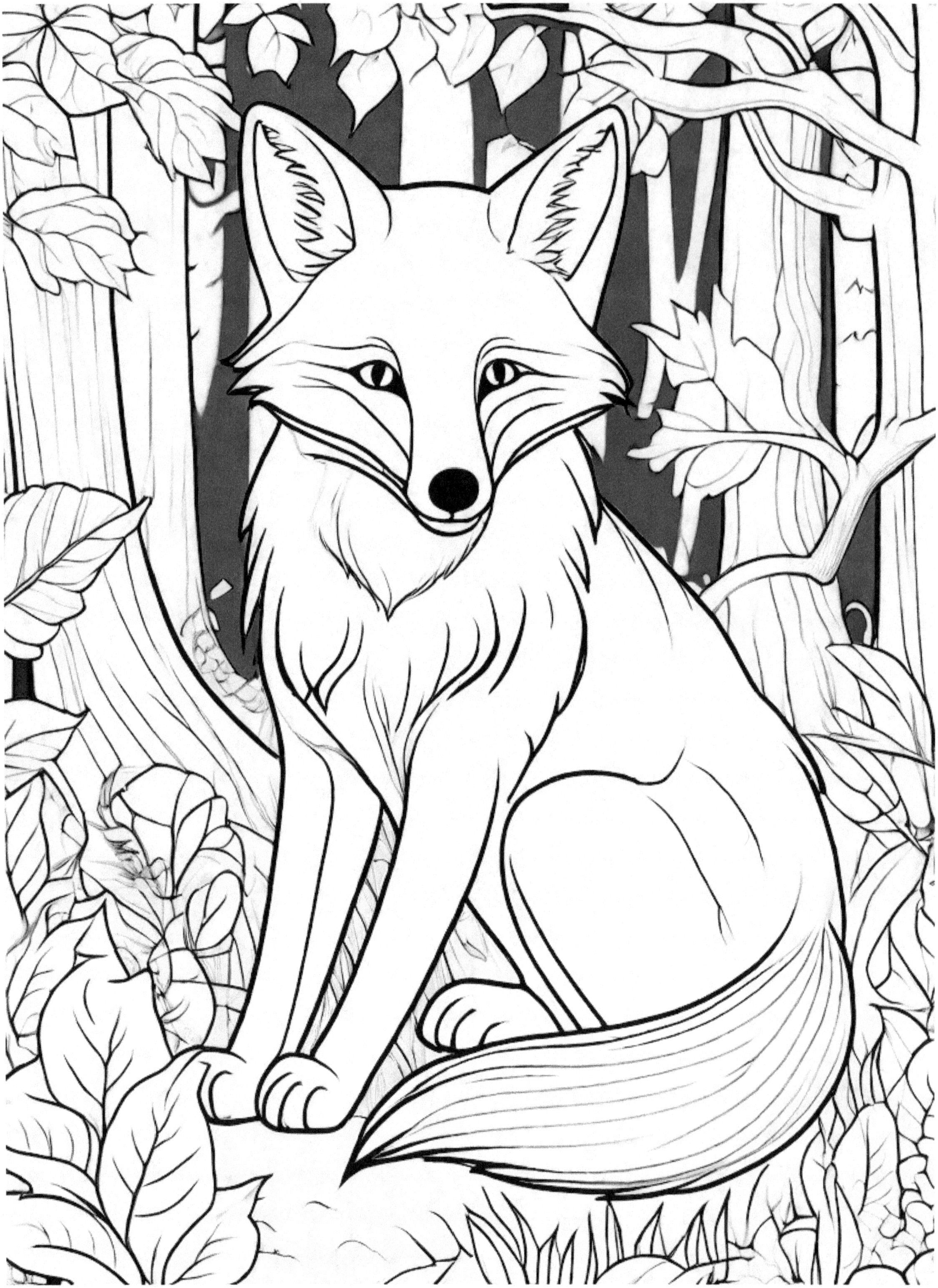

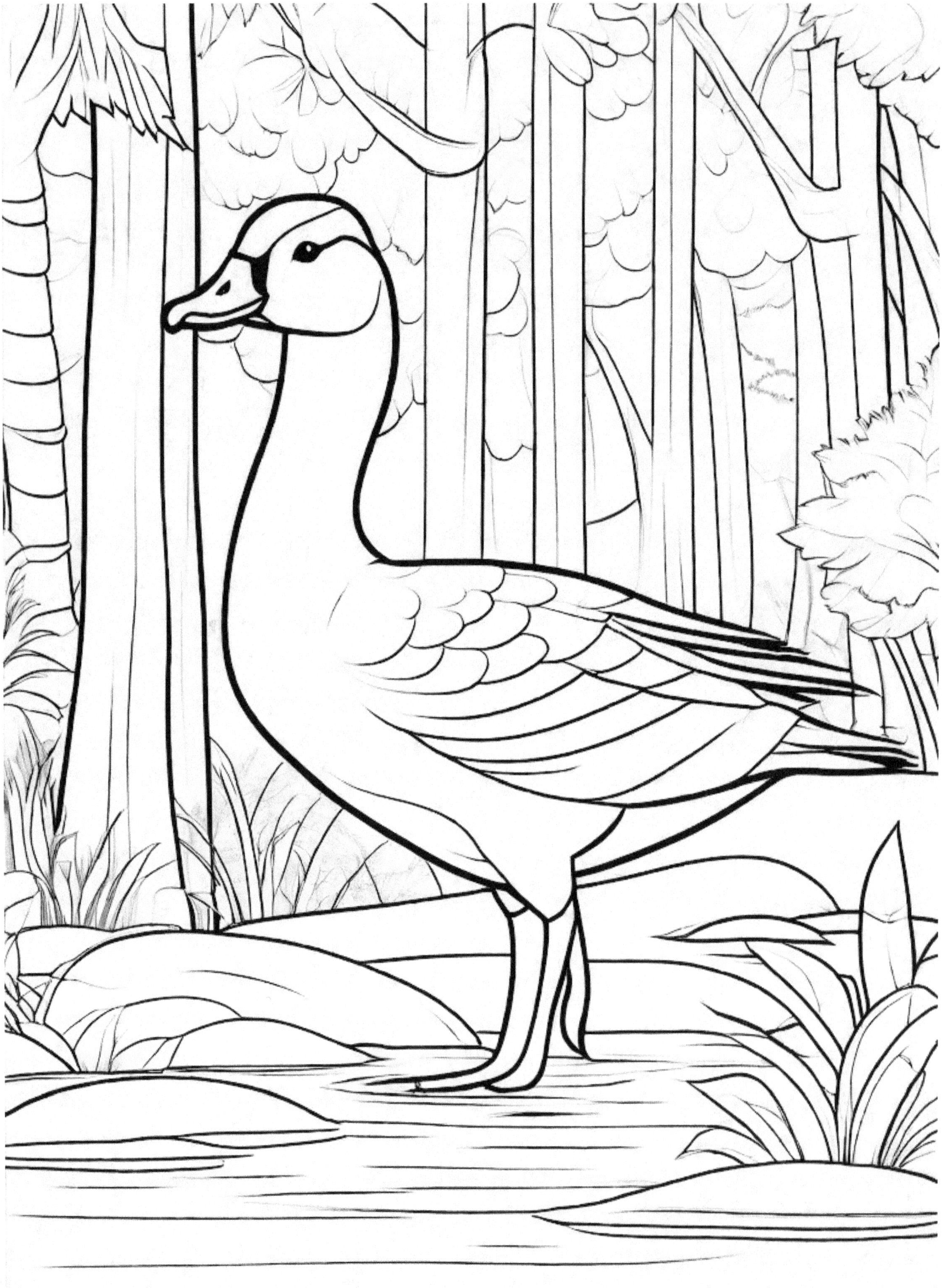

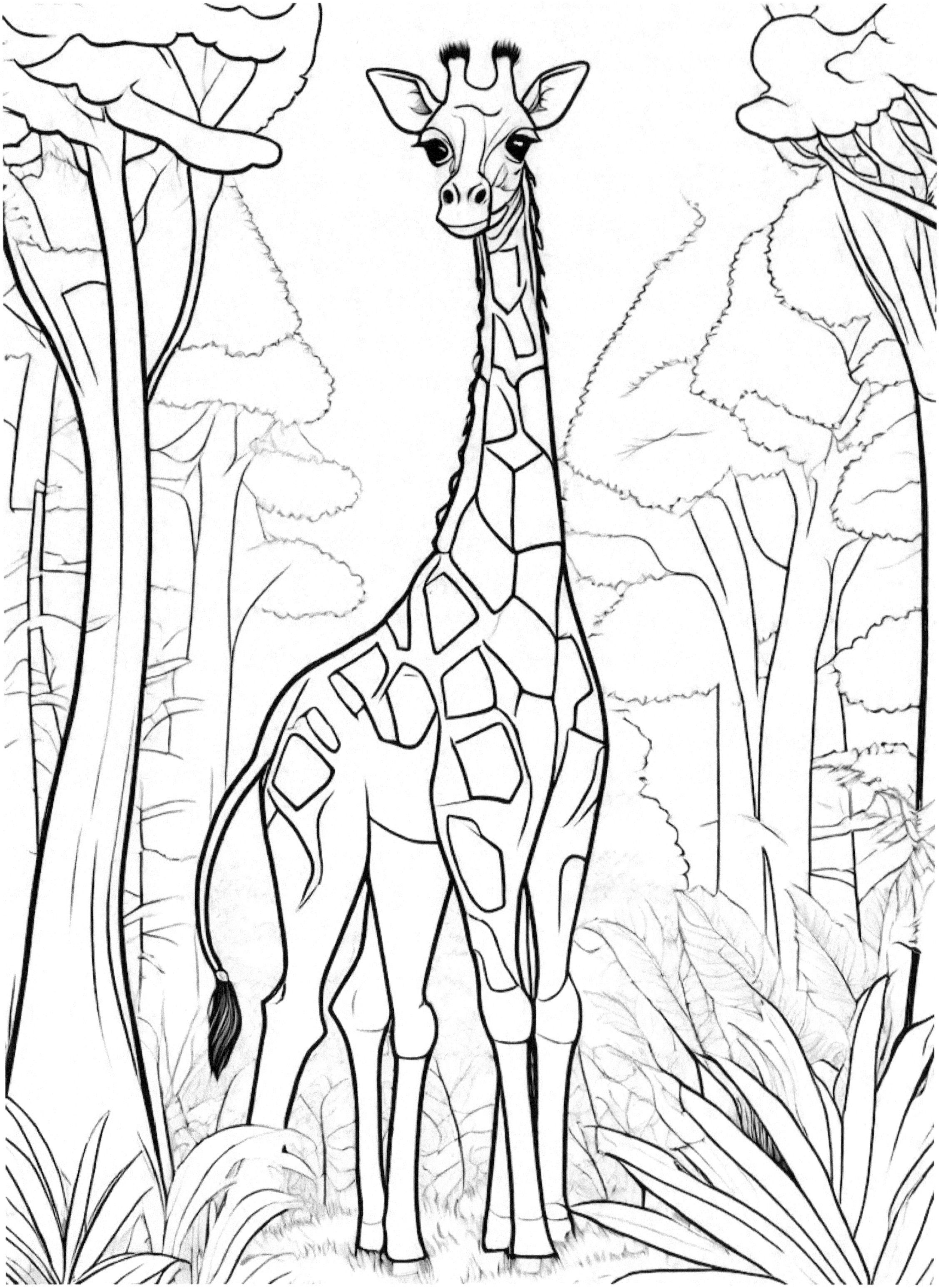

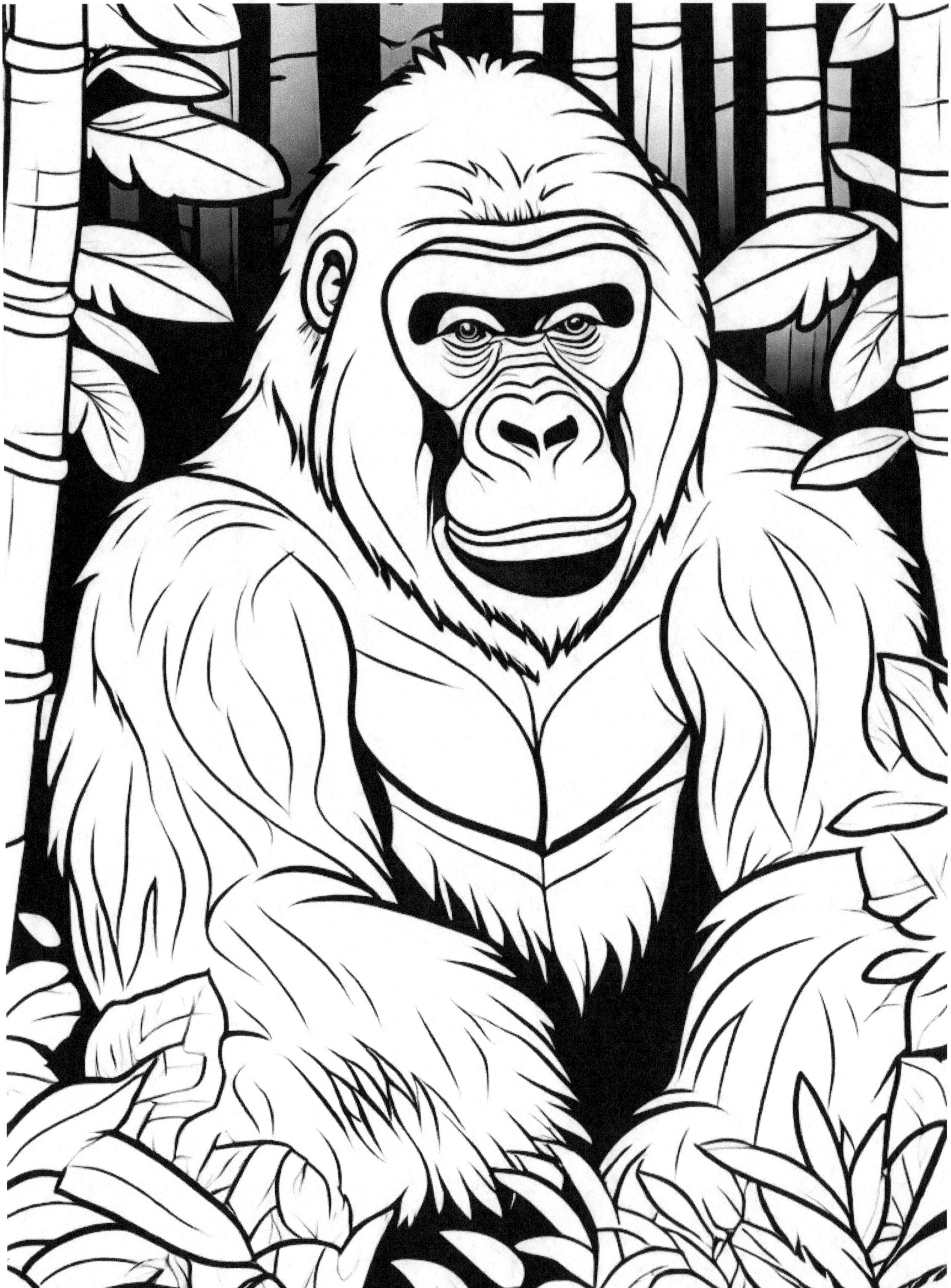

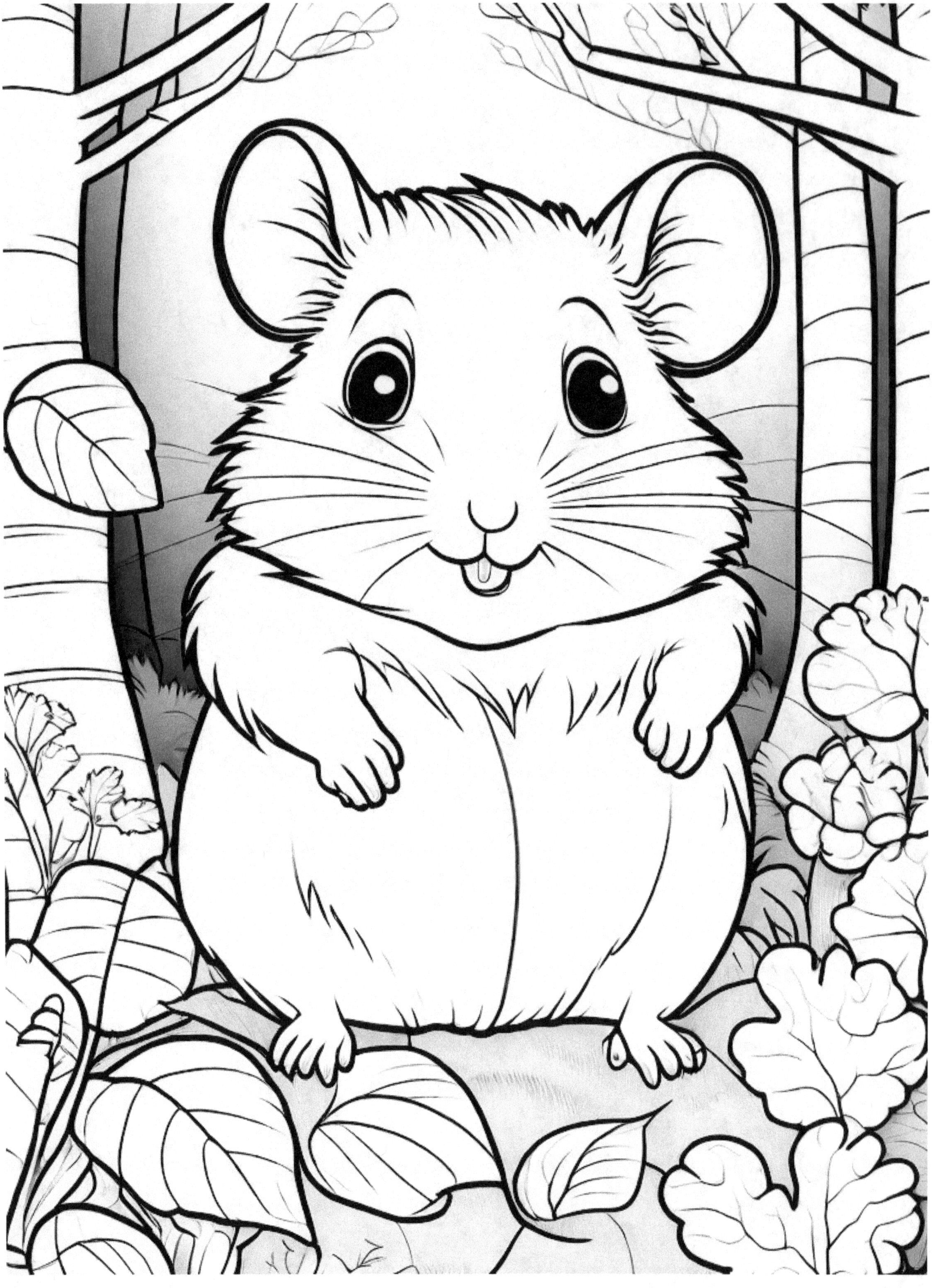

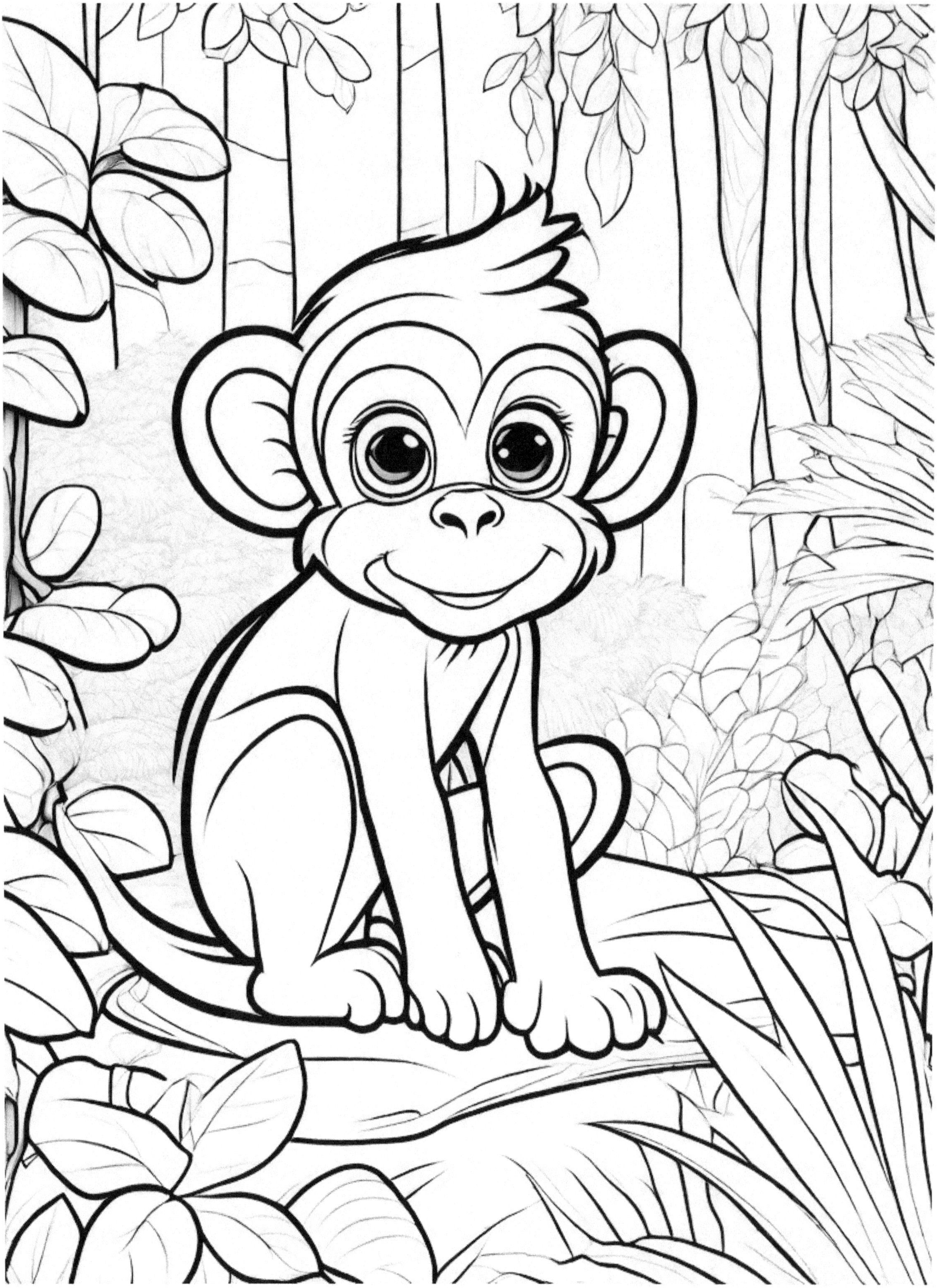

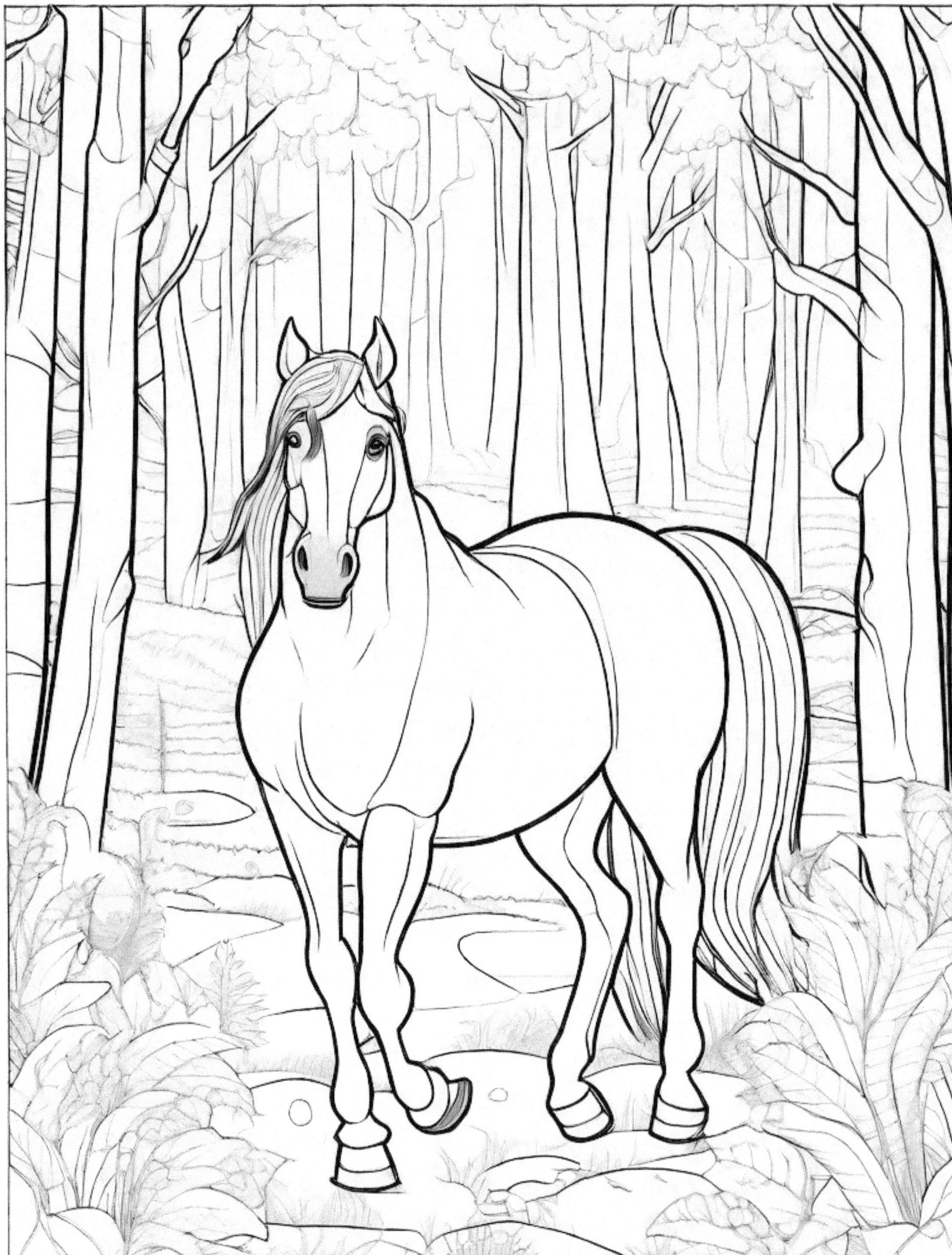

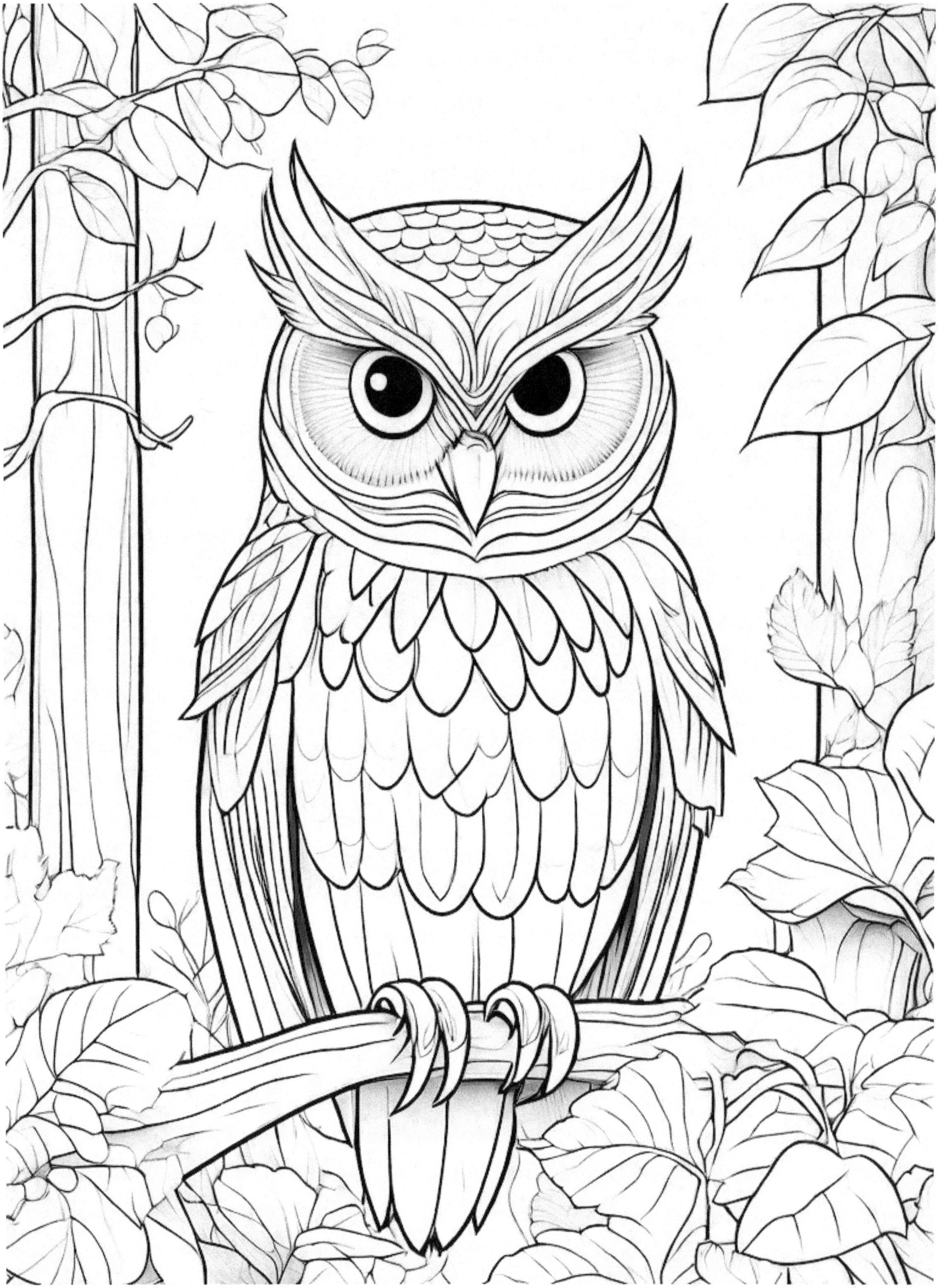

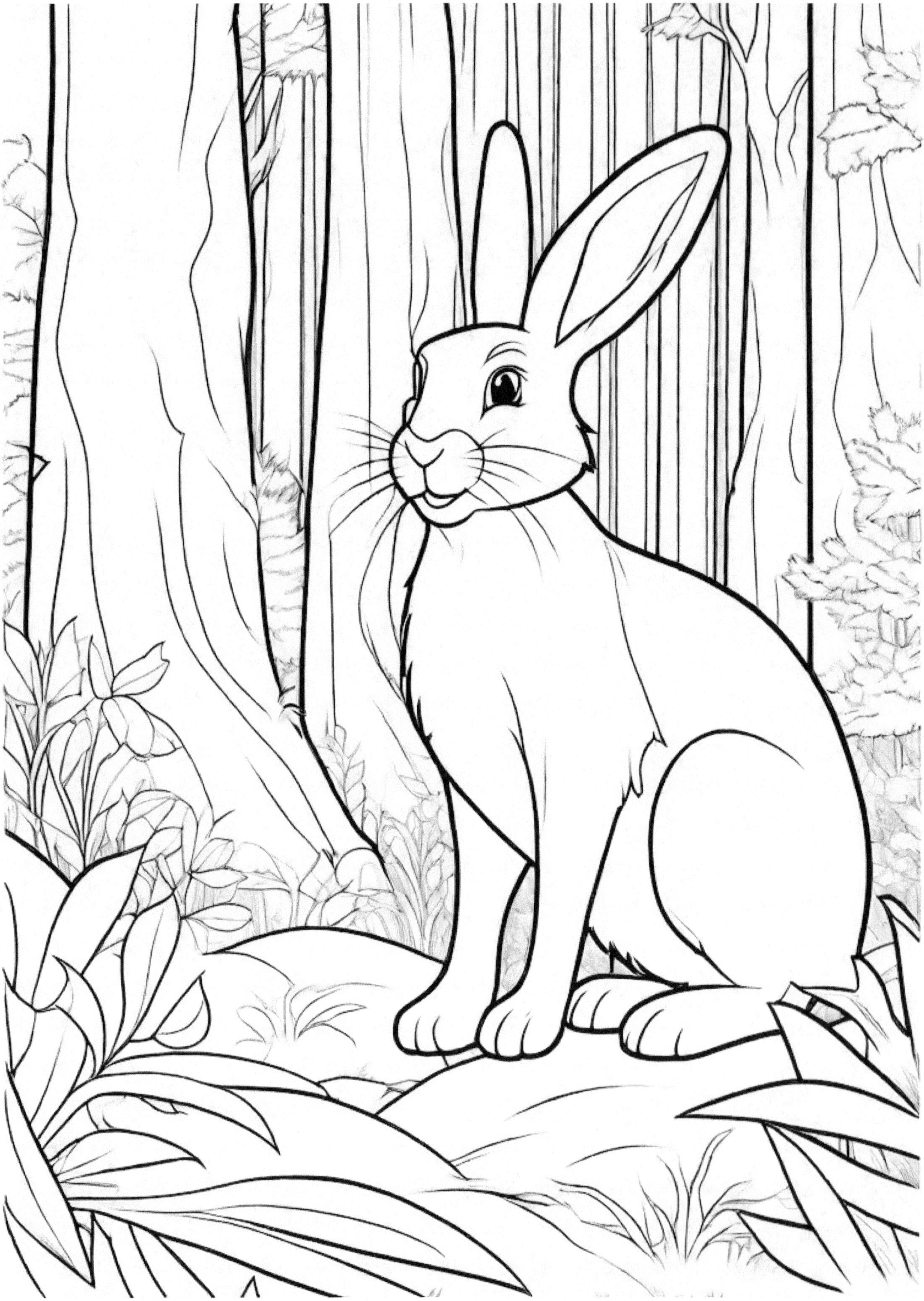

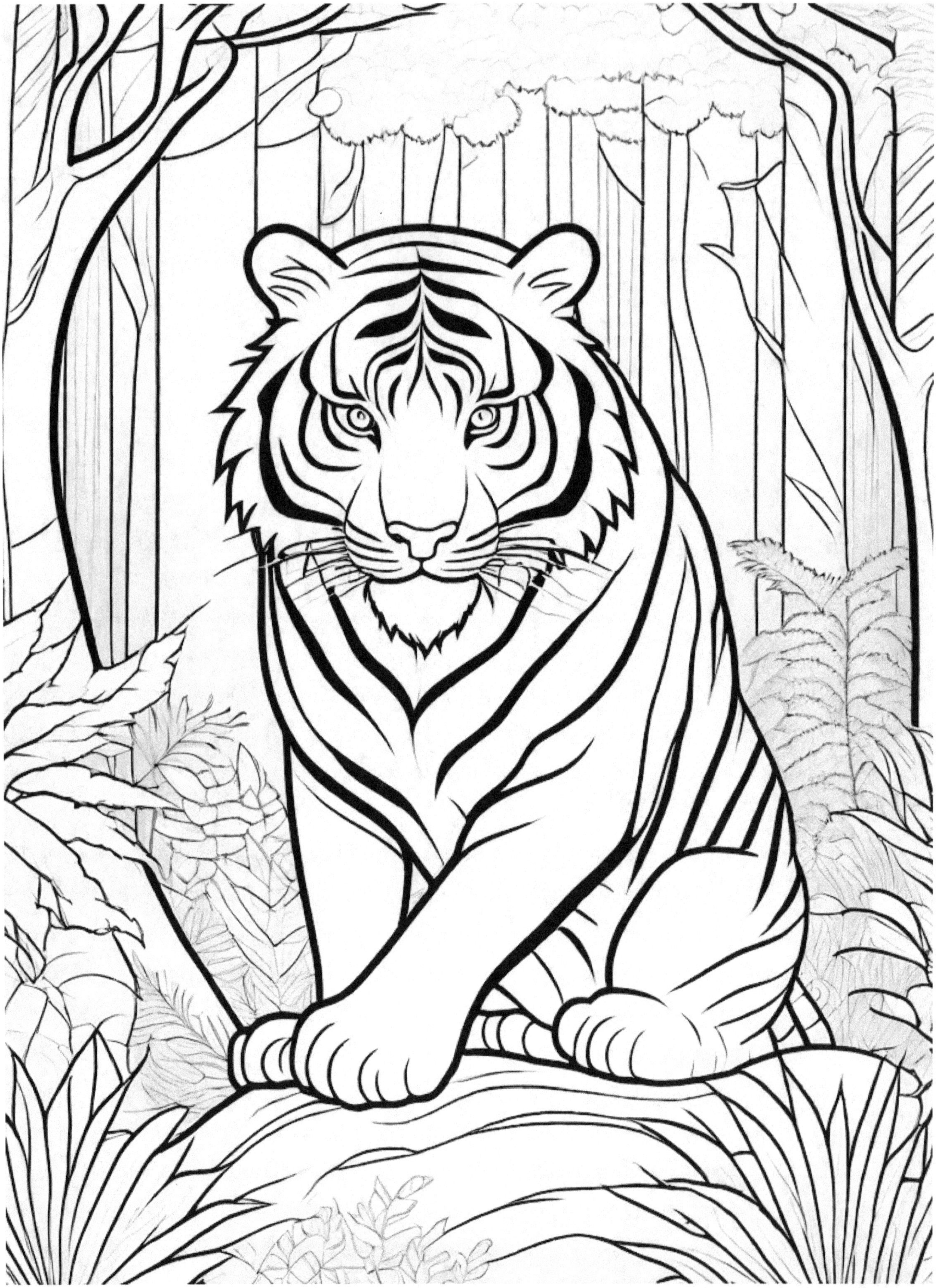

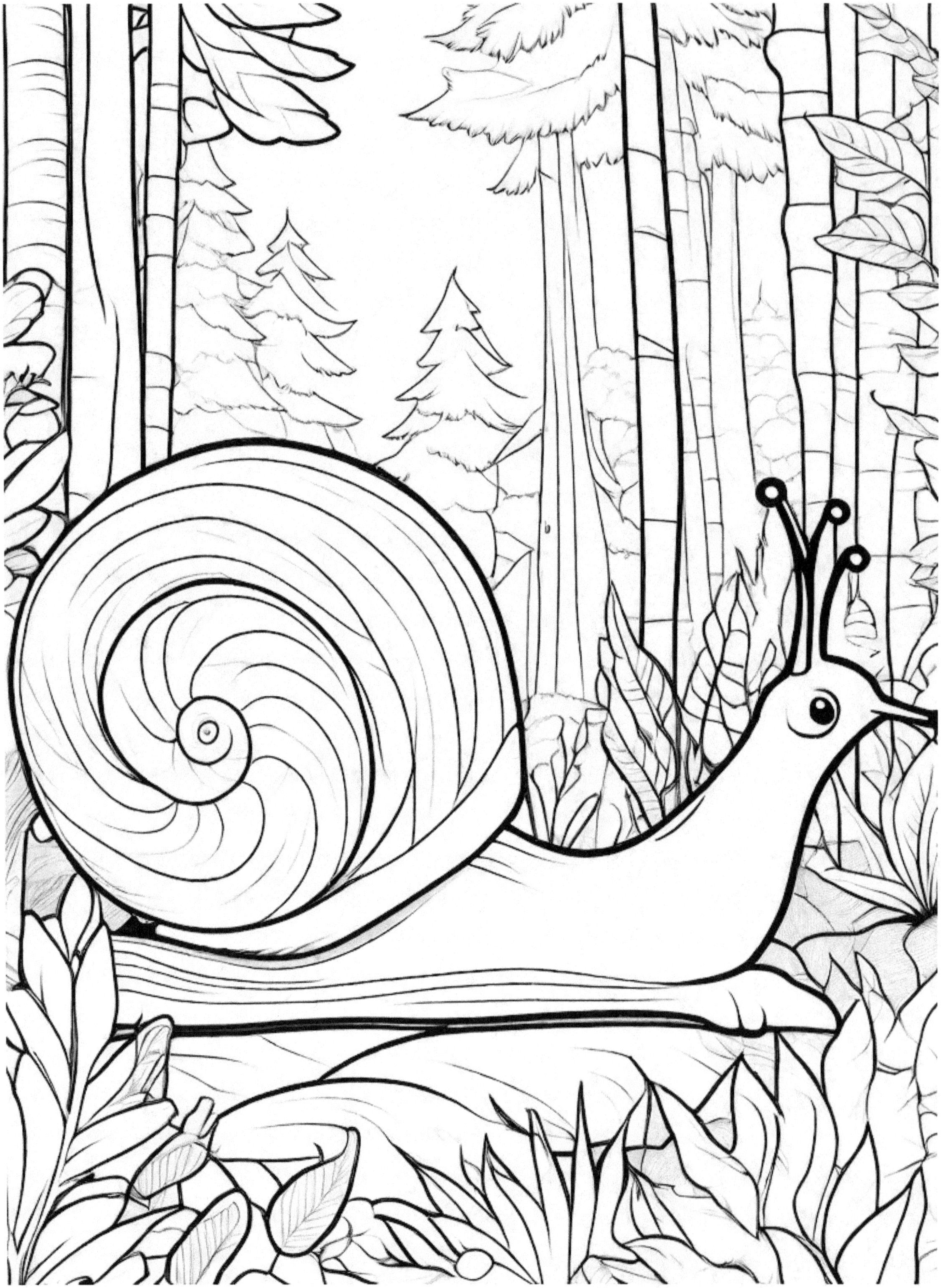

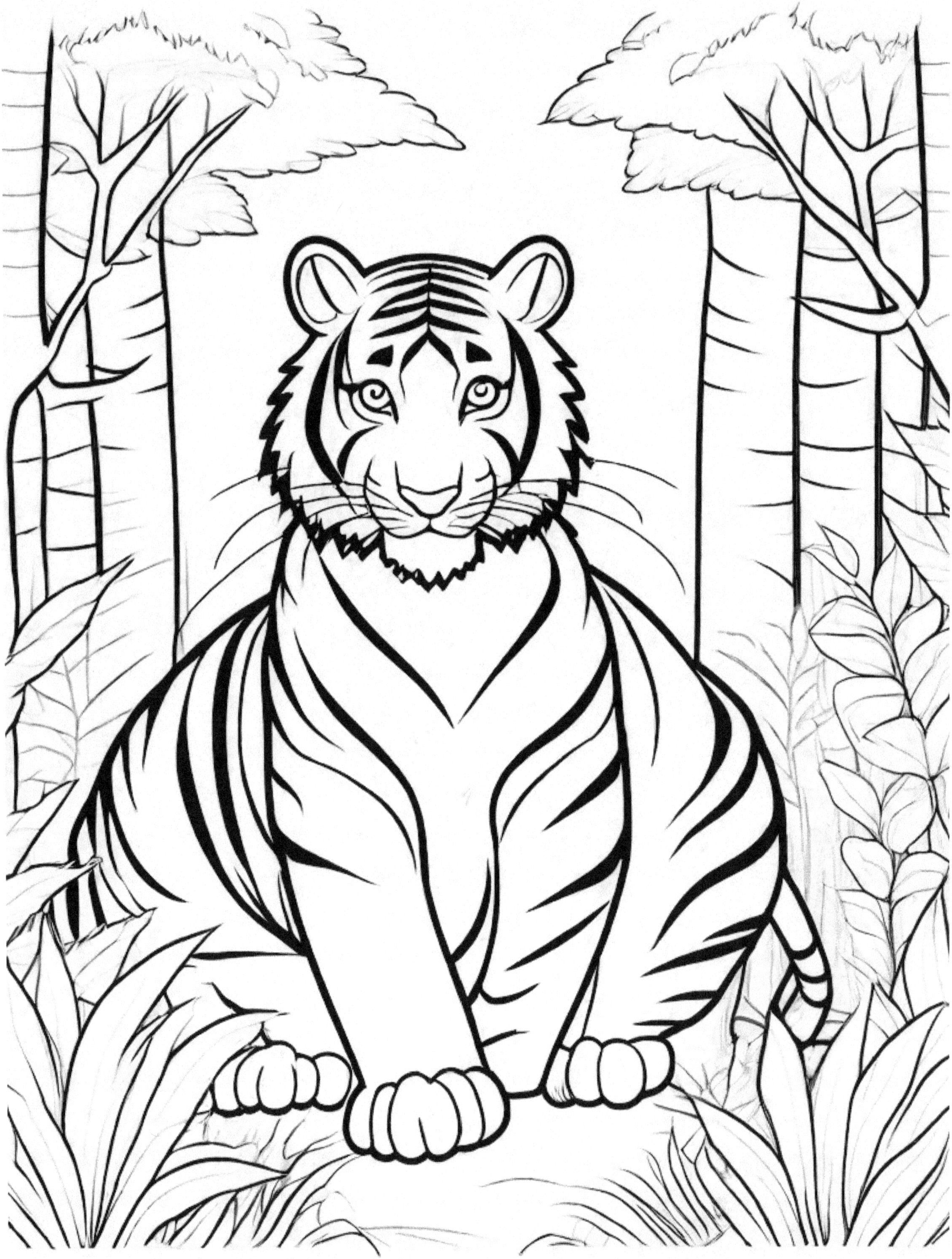

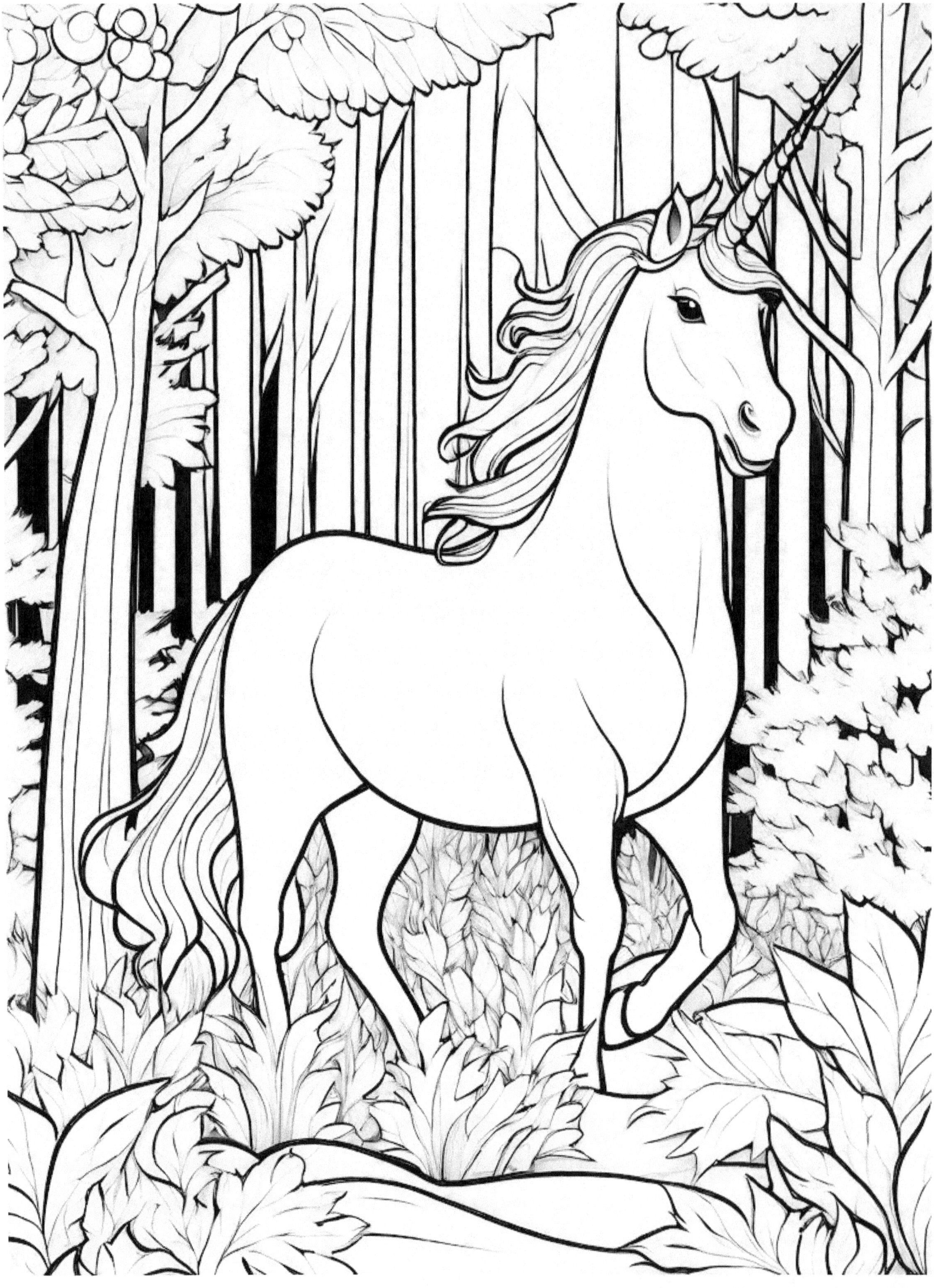

www.ingramcontent.com/pod-product-compliance
Lightning Source LLC
Chambersburg PA
CBHW082216220526
45470CB00010B/3196
* 9 7 9 8 3 2 4 9 5 4 8 6 4 *